P9-DZX-874

CLEAN FOOD

CLEAN FOOD

A SEASONAL GUIDE TO EATING CLOSE TO THE SOURCE

WITH MORE THAN 200 RECIPES
FOR A HEALTHY AND SUSTAINABLE YOU

TERRY WALTERS

STERLING EPICURE
An imprint of Sterling Publishing Co., Inc.

New York / London
www.sterlingpublishing.com

Original edition designed by MacKenzie Brown Design
Chicago, Illinois
www.mackenziebrown.com

Artwork by Donna Estabrooks
Florence, Massachusetts
www.donnaestabrooks.com

This book is FSC Chain-of-Custody certified and has been printed and bound in a sustainable manner using recycled materials and agri-based inks.

STERLING and the distinctive Sterling logo are registered trademarks of Sterling Publishing Co., Inc.

Library of Congress Cataloging-in-Publication Data

Walters, Terry
  Clean food : a seasonal guide to eating close to the source with more than 200 recipes
for a healthy and sustainable you / Terry Walters.   .
      p. cm.
  Includes bibliographical references and index.
  ISBN 978-1-4027-6814-9 (hc-trade cloth : alk. paper)
  1. Vegan cookery. 2. Natural foods. I. Title.
  TX837.W2755 2009
  641.5'636--dc22
                                    2009010149
10 9 8 7 6 5 4 3

Published in 2009 by Sterling Publishing Co., Inc.
387 Park Avenue South, New York, NY 10016

Originally published in 2007
by Terry Walters, PO Box 164, Avon, CT 06001

Distributed in Canada by Sterling Publishing
c/o Canadian Manda Group, 165 Dufferin Street
Toronto, Ontario, Canada M6K 3H6
Distributed in the United Kingdom by GMC Distribution Services
Castle Place, 166 High Street, Lewes, East Sussex, England BN7 1XU
Distributed in Australia by Capricorn Link (Australia) Pty. Ltd.
P.O. Box 704, Windsor, NSW 2756, Australia

Sterling ISBN 978-1-4027-6814-9

For information about custom editions, special sales, premium and corporate purchases, please contact Sterling Special Sales Department at 800-805-5489 or specialsales@sterlingpublishing.com.

Dedicated with love
to Chip, Sarah and Sydney,
for bringing sunshine to my life
every day of every season.

Acknowledgments

My sincerest thanks to all of the women and men who have graced my kitchen and my life with their search for knowledge, for community and for support. Your energy nourishes and inspires me to continue on this journey.

To Mike Kandefer, Tony Norris and the entire Urban Oaks Organic Farm crew for your passion, your friendship and for raising some of the most delicious organic produce available.

To Jerilyn Brownstein, Rebbie Epstein, Beth Zapatka, Maria Uzzi, Nancy Frodermann, Susan Case, Robin Fierston and Jamie November-Zeff whose friendships fill my world, who dare to tell me the truth and who are there with me every step of the way, even when I'm walking alone.

To Peter Uzzi, Sue Davies and the entire Stony Corners Running Team who inspire me, who keep me running and who have carried me through miles I did not think I could endure.

To Pam Powell for sharing the passion and vision, for living with integrity and strength, for endless hours of proofing and guidance, and for her friendship, support and love (for me and my whole family). To Gary Jacobs, for filling my life with art, with music and with your friendship and respect. To Fernanda and David Jacobs, for teaching me to sprint up the hills and recover on the other side and for supporting me and my family.

To Michael Zudonyi for setting the standard for sharing a meal, an evening and a life with warmth, beauty and love. To Rosanne Demanski, who helps me create a healthier future.

To Bill Case, lawyer extraordinaire, who closed one door and opened up a world of opportunity.

To my agent, Tony Gardner, who took me under his wing and became my friend, my mentor and my tour guide on this adventure of a lifetime. You are a blessing.

To Marcus Leaver, Marisa Bulzone, Leigh Ann Ambrosi, Meaghan Finnerty and the entire *Clean Food* team at Sterling Publishing, who connected with my vision from day one and have honored me every day of this project with their support, guidance and partnership. Thank you for believing in me and helping me create a cleaner future.

To Steve Riggio, who will never know how much his online book order meant to me.

To Lynda Moecker, for your wisdom, guidance, enthusiasm and for your help making it *clean* in the final hour. And to Paul Elledge, who can take my picture anytime.

To Donna Estabrooks, whose art graces the pages of this book as well as the walls of my home. Every time I am drawn into your work I am reminded that food is just one form of nourishment, and that living in full color with passion and truth is essential for a healthy, vibrant life.

To MacKenzie Brown Design for your vision and creativity and for listening to my heart and designing a book that expresses my soul even better than I can. To Kurt MacKenzie, to Tammy Nakashima — my deepest gratitude. And to Andrew Brown who insisted that it would kill him NOT to do this book. Thank you for sharing your talent and making mine look better, for your generosity and sense of humor and for being my friend and my family.

Finally, I can't imagine where I would be today without the following people who not only make my life, but are my life. To my mother whose commitment to healthy living is an inspiration, who puts me first even before herself and who will eat anything I cook and love it without question. To my father, and greatest fan, who teaches me by his example how to think critically, live ethically and believe what's in my heart.

To Chip, the man who married a girl I hardly remember, who has eaten quinoa and kale for decades when his very essence calls out for steak and potatoes (or at least Ben & Jerry's), who has shared with me more pain than I ever imagined and more joy than I knew possible, who makes me laugh so hard I cry, and who fills my heart with his honor, respect, pride and love.

And, to Sarah and Sydney, my greatest creations of all, from whom I learn every day. Thank you for your patience and for sharing this journey. You are my inspiration and the gifts of a lifetime.

Contents

When my mother put dinner on the table, it was a well-orchestrated affair. She insisted on clean food – rich in protein, fiber, vitamins and minerals – a virtual symphony of colors and tastes all of which occurred naturally. Our food was not altered with additives, growth hormones or pesticides, and our meals were made from scratch with natural ingredients, with intention and with love. Every evening the family sat around the table and infused our meals with laughter, mischief, conversation, and most importantly, connection. We did not eat perfect diets, nor were we a model family, but we were nourished and nurtured by wholesome foods, the energy and love that was cooked into them and by the ritual of mealtime.

My Mother's Kitchen

Over the years, my mother's meals have changed. Natural meats and dairy products have been replaced with organic black beans and kale, chicken and eggs with miso and wild Alaskan salmon, bread and butter with quinoa and extra virgin olive oil. I nourish myself with a balanced diet of locally grown, organic, unprocessed foods prepared fresh daily. Yet, when I am in my mother's home, there is a force that pulls me to explore her refrigerator and cupboards.

If hunger and nutrition are not what drive me to scavenge through my mother's kitchen, what is it that I'm searching for? Could it be the same thing I search for after the children are in bed and I am drawn to my own kitchen to find that elusive little something that's going to make me feel complete?

In this country, the topic of food is charged with emotion and controversy. The whole meals of my past are now an illusion. Nothing is as it appears on the surface. Our produce departments and grocery shelves are lined with unknowns – pesticides, herbicides, growth hormones, chemical additives and process upon process, stripping our food of its inherent nutritional value. Behind each glass of milk or piece of meat is an agenda, a lobbyist, a Fortune 500 company, a distribution chain, a processing plant... you need to squint to see the farmer and you need binoculars to find the cow!

The further we remove ourselves from the source of our food, the less we are able to maintain physical and emotional balance. Our processed food diets are so lacking in nutrition that we require coffee to wake up, sugar to get through the day, television to calm down, alcohol to let go of our inhibitions, chocolate and ice cream to feel satisfied, pills to sleep through the night and drugs to provide us with the illusion of health. The vitamins and nutrients that were so rich in my mother's whole meals are hard to come by, and the nourishment from that mealtime is even more rare. Have we become a society that is artificially sustained?

Perhaps what I am searching for in my mother's kitchen is not in the food at all. Perhaps the craving that never seems satisfied is actually a desire for connection, for mealtime.

The more we eliminate processed foods from our diets, the more aware we become of our physical and emotional being. And yet, a perfect diet alone will not fully nourish us. What we need is connection – to our bodies, hearts and spirits, to our families, to community, the environment, the land, the season and to a purpose. That is what my mother created around our kitchen table, what I strive to create around mine and what I hope to help you create around yours.

There are no nutritional supplements that will replace the love and good intention infused in a home-cooked meal. The cleaner we eat, the clearer we think, and the better we can embrace good health and nutrition. I hope that this book inspires and empowers you to nourish yourself with delicious, healthy, balanced meals. I wish for you the fulfillment of a greater connection with your environment, your community and, most importantly, yourself.

Terry

A Universal Approach to Diet

Bestseller books on diet, nutrition and wellness flood the shelves of bookstores offering a variety of approaches and much to consider. While many of these authors have discovered the diet that works perfectly for *them*, that does not mean their approach will work perfectly for *you*. However, the more knowledge we gain, the more empowered we become to tap in to the nutritionist within and to serve our own unique needs.

What we need is a master formula that takes everything into consideration – season, environment, metabolism, activity level, stress, hormonal activity, alkalinity, age, sex. There are so many factors that come into play, and just when we think we've got the answers, our bodies go and change! Ultimately, the best way to serve our unique nutritional needs is to empower ourselves with knowledge, listen to our bodies and respond with healthy, nourishing choices.

To do this, we need to realize that we have choices in the first place. A little knowledge goes a long way. Without it, we are vulnerable to deceptive marketing and labeling, and easily influenced by time-saving cooking techniques and appliances that diminish the nutritional value of our food and that can introduce harmful elements.

Consider not only the source of your food but the consequences to your health. Shiny red tomatoes in winter lure us in with their novelty, but where do they come from? The source of those tomatoes is a warm, sunny, faraway place. To withstand the long journey from farm to shelf and continue to look fresh and perfect, even I would need to be artificially enhanced! And what if I eat that "modified" tomato? It won't help me stay warm in winter, nor will it provide the nutrients that I got from the fresh local tomatoes just months earlier. **For maximum nutrition, we're better off eating closer to the source and relying on Mother Nature for seasonal produce to keep us in balance.**

Intention is equally difficult to cultivate and just as important when it comes to improving health. Before you walk into a grocery store, a restaurant or even your own kitchen, pause, take a deep breath and connect with the intention to select only foods that serve you. The goal is to say no to the junk and fill the pantry and your body with healthy foods. If you make the healthier choice at the store, you won't be faced with making it every time you open your pantry!

The final step is to suspend our judgments about food and nutrition. Perhaps you believe that fat is a four-letter word or that certain foods are more appealing for one meal over another. These notions can be handed down to us or passed on through marketing and industry. Cereal and toast may be an easy grab in the morning, but do they really provide the complete nutrition we need to get through the day? You may never eat meat again or you may never stop, but would your more nutritionally balanced dinner fuel you better if you ate it for breakfast?

For many, health improvements can be accomplished by improving habits, reducing stress on our bodies and increasing efficiency. All in all, the more you know about your food and your body, the more easily you can distinguish the foods and habits that harm from those that heal, and the more successful you can be at maintaining health and balance.

The seasons are what a symphony ought to be:
four perfect movements in harmony with each other.

ARTHUR RUBENSTEIN

A Cleaner and Healthier Way

It's time to erase the line between nutrition and nourishment! Clean food is minimally processed, so our bodies get the maximum nutritional value needed to fuel metabolism. The more clean food we bring in, the cleaner and more efficiently our bodies function. But, maintaining good health encompasses much more than clean food. True nourishment must feed our unique constitutions, and fulfill our emotional and spiritual needs. In our fast-paced culture this holistic approach is frequently overlooked and undervalued. It's time to look within for the answers.

Eating clean is a great way to make healthy dietary choices, but significant health benefits can also be achieved simply by slowing down. The results are less mental and physical stress, more oxygen circulating through the body, more toxins eliminated, more strength and more efficiency of nearly every system. Imagine how tired your organs must be from keeping up with your fast pace, not to mention your fast food!

Here's an easy exercise to incorporate into each day:

DAILY MEDITATION

Take five minutes and sit in a quiet place. Close your eyes and focus on your breath. Let your shoulders drop. Relax your facial muscles. Breathe into your belly. Turn off the conversations in your head. Notice how your breath starts to slow down and deepen. Slowly increase the duration of your session until you are comfortably meditating for 30 minutes a day. From this place of stillness, you are more in tune with your whole being, and improved balance and health are possible.

To truly nourish ourselves, we need this healing stillness, as well as an understanding of how we fuel our activity and how we are affected by the foods we eat. Does a bagel for breakfast make you feel sluggish? Can a bowl of oatmeal keep you running strong for hours? Maybe you opt for coffee instead of breakfast or a snack instead of lunch. Are you dragging by the end of the day?

You can't drive your car all day with no gas in the tank and then stop to fill up on the way home. Yet we expect our bodies to operate exactly this way.

One way to achieve greater understanding of your body is to keep a journal. Record what you eat, when you eat it and how you feel throughout the day. Check in with yourself for one day, two days or a week. I find the change of season to be the perfect time for this kind of introspection. Include everything from mood, sleep patterns, energy levels and digestive issues to menstrual symptoms, headaches, exercise regimen and more.

The more thoroughly you journal, the more insight you will gain into your physical and emotional being. Patterns will reveal themselves, and the foods and habits that nourish you (and those that don't) will become apparent. This awareness is essential for becoming empowered to make positive changes in your health and in your life.

By slowing down, experimenting with different foods and food combinations and paying greater attention to your body's responses, YOU can become your own "in-house nutritionist."

SAMPLE FOOD JOURNAL		
DAILY ACTIVITY AND DIET	TIME OF DAY	EMOTIONAL AND PHYSICAL OUTCOMES
WAKE UP 8 oz. water Walk the dog – 25 mins. Black coffee, bagel with cream cheese	6:30 AM	Didn't sleep well. Several trips to the bathroom. Difficulty getting started.
	7:30 AM	
	8:30 AM	Feeling better
WORK 8 oz. water Coffee, cream and sugar	9:30 AM	Focused
	10:30 AM	
	11:30 AM	Hungry; feeling worn out
GET LUNCH Green salad and grilled chicken	12:30 PM	Not productive, bad mood
	1:30 PM	Much more energy
Can of cola and a nutrition bar	2:30 PM	Tired, dragging, hard time focusing, slight headache
	3:30 PM	
GO TO GYM Workout – 1 hr	4:30 PM	Feel a bit more energy and better mood
	5:30 PM	
HOME Late dinner – pasta with vegetables, salad and bread. Snack on cheese while making dinner.	6:30 PM	Insatiable appetite
	7:30 PM	Bloated after dinner
	8:30 PM	Tired, low energy
Chocolate	9:30 PM	Unsatisfied
8 oz. water	10:30 PM	Hard time staying awake to watch TV
TO BED	11:30 PM	

Clean Food

It's hard to believe how far we've strayed from real food. Our grocery stores overflow with foods that can last on the shelves for months. So much of our food supply is stripped of its goodness and pumped full of man-made taste, color and nutrients. It's no wonder our health continues to deteriorate.

I find that my youngest students grasp the concept of clean food the best. Together we examine a bowl of plain brown rice and a box of quick-cooking vegetable rice pilaf. They tell me what they think is in each container. "Protein, starch, carbohydrates!" they shout. We pick up the box and start reading. The first few ingredients are identifiable. Then we get into what seems like another language – poly-this, hydrogenated-that, artificial, high-fructose, modified, mono- and di-. We consider the brown rice. There is no label – a clear sign of being closer to the source. What you see is what you get – brown rice. The conclusion is easy. If you can read it or imagine how it grows, it's clean. If you can't, neither can your body. You're better off without! Clean food is naturally grown and minimally processed.

The diagram below uses oats to illustrate how our foods move from a "whole" and nutritious state (on the left) to a highly processed and nutritionally depleted state (on the right). Similarly, a head of broccoli grows from the earth and becomes processed as it is cut, steamed, sautéed, dehydrated, ground and possibly even added to that very package of instant vegetable rice pilaf.

The nutritional value of that head of broccoli and its effect on our health and well-being change throughout the different stages of processing. We know that broccoli is full of chlorophyll, calcium and vitamins. Eaten raw, steamed, quick boiled, blanched or even flash frozen, broccoli retains much of its nutritional goodness. Once processed, either in a processing plant or your own microwave oven, as much as 90 percent of that goodness can be lost. That does not mean that you need to eat broccoli raw to access its nutritional value. In fact, *your* body may be able to assimilate more of the nutrients and digest it better if it is lightly steamed or sautéed.

What we know for sure is that the more our food is processed, the more its natural nutrients are lost. This means that the best way to nourish ourselves is with clean food eaten as close to the source as possible. No matter where your foods fall on this chart, one step to the left can yield health benefits. Smaller steps and slower change are the keys to an easy and successful transition.

Most Natural and Nutritious State
CLEAN FOOD

Least Nutritious State
HIGHLY PROCESSED FOODS

◄ ·· ►

| Whole Oat Groats | Steel Cut Oats | Rolled Oats | Quick Cooking Oats | Instant Oatmeal | Packaged Cold Cereal |

Only you know where the foods you eat fall on the chart from clean to processed foods, and in the end, only you can make healthier choices and follow a cleaner, healthier path.

Eating for Balance

Regularly I'm asked what kind of diet I follow: vegetarian, vegan, macrobiotic, raw foods, and so on. No matter how you eat, inevitably, someone will want to put a label on you. We try diets like we try hairstyles and the possibilities are infinite, but are we well served by adhering to one defined, and perhaps limited, approach to eating?

Webster's dictionary defines diet as "food and drink regularly provided or consumed, habitual nourishment." Lasting changes and health improvements are not found in fad diets. They are achieved by listening to your body, making healthy choices in diet and exercise to achieve balance on a daily basis, eating as cleanly as possible and discovering the formula that best serves your unique composition.

For years, I thought I needed to have an advanced degree in medicine to figure out balanced nutrition. How much protein do I need? Are carbohydrates good or bad? Am I getting all my vitamins? Am I getting enough calcium and minerals? The truth is, balanced nutrition can be easy and requires just a little knowledge to start you on your way.

For most of us, eating clean is not as much a matter of learning what to eat, as it is of applying what we already know. Adults and children alike can apply the following concepts to make healthy choices, eat a balanced diet and enjoy good health all year long.

Eat…

…all the colors of the rainbow

…all five tastes*

…a varied diet

…locally grown, seasonal foods

and

Enjoy your food and mealtime.

*See page 9

Ways to Improve Health and Well-being

While the concepts below may seem simple, the cumulative effect of ignoring them creates excess stress on the body, contributes to acidity and becomes the basis of imbalance and disease. I find that life has a way of pulling me away from these ideals, and an occasional review is a helpful way to get back on track.

1. Chew, Chew, Chew!

The more you chew, the slower you eat, the more digestive enzymes you secrete, the less stress on your digestive organs, the more nutrients you absorb from your food, the more easily you eliminate. . . I've known people to shed pounds simply by increasing their chewing.

2. Practice Good Habits

Take the time to sit down when you eat so you have more energy for proper digestion and nutrient absorption. We also need to eat regular meals to fuel our metabolism and daily activities. The more we practice good habits, the more automatic they become and the better an example we set for our children and others.

3. Stop Eating Three Hours Before Bedtime

Digestion is directly linked to movement and exercise. When we sleep, everything slows down – including our digestive functions. If you go to sleep with food in your belly, your mind may sleep, but your body works overtime all night long. Over the long term, this regimen makes the body weak, out of balance and less able to maintain good health.

4. Don't Buy It If You Don't Want to Eat It

It's much easier to have strength and willpower once (in the grocery store) than every time you open up your cupboard! Do yourself a favor – fill your kitchen with nourishing foods so that you can't help but make a healthy choice.

5. Color + Taste = Balance

A balanced diet includes a full spectrum of color (not just white) and all five tastes: SWEET, SOUR, SALTY, PUNGENT and BITTER. Go for variety and start adding tastes and colors that have been missing from your palette. Make sure to put extra emphasis on green – the color of healing.

6. Listen To and Honor Your Body

At the end of the day, as you rummage through the kitchen looking for the perfect snack to fill that elusive need, ask yourself, "Am I hungry or thirsty, or do I need connection, touch, an emotional outlet, some pampering or sleep?" Answer these questions instead of reaching for the snack and discover how to truly nourish and nurture your inner self. Sometimes a massage, a foot bath, time alone with a journal or early to bed will do the trick; other times a bite of chocolate is simply the only answer!

7. Change Slowly

Go easy on your body, your lifestyle and even your sense of taste. Too big a jump from processed to unprocessed foods can bring uncomfortable side effects. Changes made too quickly can put added stress on the body and are more likely to backfire. Gradual changes allow your body and your life to adapt more easily and are more likely to be long lasting.

8. Make Peace with Your Food and Your Choices

Ultimately, life is just a series of choices – one at a time. Every choice nourishes some part of us – whether physical or emotional. The goal is to accurately identify the need and then nourish it as best as possible. The more ways we have to nourish ourselves, the less we use (and misuse) food, and the happier and healthier we can be.

9. Let Go

It's just food, after all. What you see isn't always what you get, and we can't make good choices unless we have good information. But overemphasis on food and diet isn't healthy either. Don't let the food control you. Put it in a healthy place, and nourish yourself lavishly with all that life has to offer.

If you've gotten this far, you've overcome the greatest hurdle of all. Holding the intention is half the battle of changing to a healthy, balanced diet. If you're unaccustomed to purchasing and preparing whole foods, you'll benefit from outfitting your kitchen with a few standard tools and familiarizing yourself with basic preparations and tips for cooking grains, legumes, vegetables, sea vegetables and more. Then you'll be able to dive into the seasonal recipes in this book with the confidence and knowledge needed to successfully prepare balanced meals rich in color, variety, taste and the nutrients essential for healthy metabolism.

Tools

Keep it simple and keep it natural! A friend once commented, "It's great to see that you don't need to have a fancy kitchen to make delicious, healthy food." She was right. Some basic tools can accomplish a variety of tasks and eliminate unwanted clutter. Shy away from single-use gadgets whose only function can be performed with a skillfully used knife. When it's time to purchase, go for quality and avoid unnatural or harmful materials such as aluminum (a known carcinogen), plastic (a petro-chemical that leaches harmful dioxins and PCBs) and Teflon.

LARGE WOOD OR BAMBOO CUTTING BOARD
At least 20 x 15 inches

THREE QUALITY KNIVES
High carbon stainless steel blades: an 8-inch chef's knife, a serrated-edge bread knife and a paring knife.

COLANDER
A large stainless steel colander will work for both pasta and vegetables.

STAINLESS STEEL STRAINER
Make sure the weave is tight enough for rinsing grains.

WOODEN SPOONS
Look for a variety of sizes and long handles.

HEAT-RESISTANT SPATULAS
While I try to avoid man-made materials, heat-resistant silicone spatulas in large and small sizes are great for scraping out a food processor or mixing bowl.

GRATER AND MICROPLANE
Make sure both are designed with handles. I like the basic box grater with 4 surface options.

RICE COOKER
The fewer the parts, the easier the cleanup. Most cost $45–$100. Be sure the interior of the bowl is not exposed aluminum.

LARGE SAUTÉ PAN
I like cast iron by Lodge. It is naturally nonstick, reasonably priced and comes preseasoned in a variety of sizes.

DUTCH OVEN CASSEROLE
I use this pot for everything – steaming, sautéing, soups and more. My favorite is the #24 (4½ quart) pot by Le Creuset.

TWO COOKIE SHEETS
Select heavy gauge metal to conduct heat evenly. Have at least one with rims to prevent spillage.

PARCHMENT PAPER
Makes any baking surface nonstick and easy to clean.

GLASS STORAGE BOWLS AND MASON JARS
In a variety of sizes, for storing everything from grains and nuts to leftovers, frozen soups and school lunches.

HANDHELD BLENDER
Look for a stainless steel shaft that is removable and dishwasher-safe with a handle that is easy to grip and operate. Use interchangeably with food processor or standing blender.

FOOD PROCESSOR
Look for a large bowl, a strong motor and a model that is easy to clean and assemble. Add specialty blades and extra bowls as needed.

WOODEN CHOPSTICKS
Perfect for stirring nut and seed butters.

Basic Cooking Methods

How you prepare your food can have as profound an effect on your state of balance as what you eat. Instinctively we desire warming soups and casseroles in the winter and cooling, raw salads and fruits in the summer. Foods that require longer cooking over higher temperatures help us keep warm and maintain balance in cold weather. The reverse is also true – raw fruits and vegetables cleanse away excess fat and keep us cool and refreshed when it's warm. If you are someone who tends to feel too hot or too cold, consider what you eat and your environment for insight into how you might start to achieve greater balance.

In the Northeast, the variety of local produce diminishes dramatically in the winter months. Sticking to local foods such as grains, legumes, winter squash, root vegetables and dark leafy greens, all of which can survive through the colder months, helps us maintain balance mentally and physically. Perhaps it is not an accident that in the season of darkness and cold, Mother Earth gives us sweet and strengthening roots and grains and uplifting dark leafy greens; and in the heat of summer, we are blessed with refreshing cucumbers, tomatoes, peaches and sweet corn.

Experiment with locally grown produce and the following cooking methods throughout the seasons to discover your perfect balance.

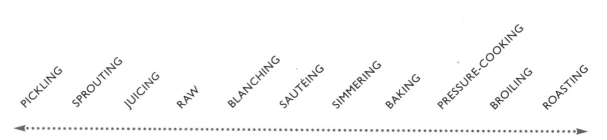

PICKLING SPROUTING JUICING RAW BLANCHING SAUTÉING SIMMERING BAKING PRESSURE-COOKING BROILING ROASTING

More Cooling   **More Warming**

Moderation is key; too much of one form of preparation can be weakening. Mix it up by adding a raw salad to your winter meal or some quick-cooking grains such as quinoa and millet to your repertoire of summer salads.

Remember, every body is different. The more you pay attention to how your body reacts, the better you will become at determining the right combination of foods and the most suitable preparation for your unique constitution.

GRAINS

Many cultures consider grains to be the most complete food and look to them as the foundation of their diets. Grains are strengthening, grounding and rich in vitamins, minerals, fiber and protein. Be aware that grains also contain phytic acid, which interferes with the absorption of zinc, calcium, iron and other essential minerals. Fortunately, phytic acid in grains is water soluble, so soak your grains for a minimum of one hour, drain, add fresh water, cook and voilà . . . the phytic acid washes away, leaving you with a significantly improved complex carbohydrate.

Even complex carbohydrates, however, create acidity in the body. To neutralize this effect and make grains more alkaline-forming, cook them together with minerals (either kombu sea vegetable or sea salt). Kombu added to grains (and legumes) during cooking also infuses them with minerals, improves digestibility, reduces gas and tenderizes. This is an easy way to amp up the nutritional value of your food.

It sounds like a lot to remember, but it quickly becomes second nature. At the end of the day, put some grain in a bowl and cover it with water. It doesn't matter if you cook the grain in the morning, the next evening, or even the day after. Simply drain, add fresh water and cook according to the instructions that follow. The longer the grain soaks, the closer it gets to germinating (sprouting), the more nutritious and easier to digest it becomes and the less water and time are required for cooking.

When selecting a grain, remember that the smaller grains such as quinoa, millet, amaranth and teff are higher in protein and free of gluten, so choose wisely and pay attention to how your body responds. If you're planning to use grain in a salad or casserole, let it sit briefly before tossing to prevent it from becoming mushy and to keep it nice and fluffy.

GRAINS

Amaranth*	Buckwheat*	Jasmine rice*	Sushi rice*
Barley (whole hulled)	Bulgur wheat	Millet*	Teff*
Brown rice* (includes short grain, medium grain, long grain, brown basmati and sweet brown rice)	Couscous (made from wheat or semolina pasta)	Oats (whole)	Wheat berries
		Quinoa*	Wild rice* (a high-protein grass that cooks up like a grain)

* Does not contain gluten

All grains can be cooked on your stovetop, but if you are like me and tend to multitask, you might find yourself reminded of your cooking grains by the smell of your burning pot! Electric rice cookers are a great invention, are reasonably priced, cook your grain perfectly every time and keep it warm until you are ready to use it.

Grains can be prepared and served simply as outlined below or as in any of the recipes throughout this book. Experiment with more water or stock to yield softer grains, and less for al dente grains. Leftover cooked grain can be stored in the refrigerator for approximately 3 days. To reheat, simply steam or water sauté.

BROWN RICE AND WHOLE OATS

1 cup uncooked grain
2 cups water or vegetable stock
Thumb-size piece kombu*

Rinse grain in strainer and place in bowl. Cover with water and soak at least 1 hour. Drain and place in pot with 2 cups fresh water or stock. Add kombu and make sure it is submerged. Cover and bring to boil. Reduce heat and simmer until liquid is absorbed (about 25 minutes). For softer texture use more water and longer cooking time. Remove from heat, remove and discard kombu, fluff and serve.

*See Sea Vegetables, page 16

WILD RICE

1 cup uncooked wild rice
2½ cups water or vegetable stock
Pinch of sea salt

Rinse wild rice in strainer and place in pot with water or stock and salt. Cover and bring to boil. Reduce heat and simmer until liquid is absorbed (35–40 minutes). For softer texture use more water and longer cooking time. Fluff and serve.

HULLED BARLEY AND WHEAT BERRIES

1 cup uncooked grain
2¼ cups water or stock
Thumb-size piece kombu

Rinse grain in strainer and place in bowl. Cover with water and soak at least 1 hour. Drain and place in pot with water or stock. Add kombu and make sure it is submerged. Cover and bring to boil. Reduce heat and simmer until liquid is absorbed (about 45 minutes). For softer texture use more water and longer cooking time. Remove from heat, remove and discard kombu, fluff and serve.

MILLET

Millet tends to be somewhat bland, so I like to pan-roast it first to bring out its nutty flavor. You can also cook your millet following the same directions as brown rice, but because millet is not an acid-forming grain, it does not require soaking.

1 cup uncooked millet
2 cups water or vegetable stock
Pinch of sea salt

Rinse millet in strainer and place in sauté pan over medium heat. Gently stir millet until it starts to give off a nutty aroma. Keeping the pan on the burner, add water or stock and salt, cover, reduce heat and simmer until all liquid is absorbed (about 25 minutes). Fluff and serve.

QUINOA
(keen-wah)

I like my quinoa to pop in my mouth when I chew it, so I cook it in less water than other grains.

1 cup uncooked quinoa
1½ cups water or vegetable stock
Thumb-size piece kombu

Rinse quinoa in strainer and place in pot with water or stock. Add kombu and make sure it is submerged. Cover and bring to boil. Reduce heat and simmer until liquid is absorbed (about 15 minutes). If you're planning to mix quinoa with vegetables, cool slightly before fluffing so it doesn't become mushy. Remove from heat, remove and discard kombu, fluff and serve.

VEGETABLES

Of all the food groups, the vegetable family has the most diversity and the greatest range of health benefits. If we divide this food group into several categories, we stand a better chance of getting a good variety of nutrients in our diets. Select from all of the vegetable categories regularly for maximum nutrition and good health.

DARK LEAFY GREENS

Rich in calcium, chlorophyll, iron and vitamins C and E, this food category is the most beneficial and the most underconsumed in our culture. Dark leafy greens lift our mood, heal our organs and counteract the damage resulting from our stressful lives. Try to add nutritionally packed greens to your diet every day. While many of these greens are part of the cabbage family, I separate them here to bring attention to what I call the heavy hitters – those that pack a big nutritional punch! Select from kale, collards, mustard greens, dandelion greens, watercress and romaine lettuce.

CRUCIFEROUS VEGETABLES

Known for their cancer-preventing nutrients and antioxidants, these vegetables break down and dissolve fats to help eliminate toxins. Here are some of the many varieties to look for: collard greens, cauliflower, broccoli, Napa cabbage, Savoy cabbage, bok choy, pac choy, tatsoi, Brussels sprouts, green and purple cabbages, daikon radish, red radishes and watermelon radishes.

ROOTS AND TUBERS

These vegetables, which dig down into the ground, help us feel strong and "rooted" and provide vitamin A, beta-carotene, minerals, fiber, antioxidants and healthy sweetness to our diets. Look for parsnips, rutabagas, turnips, ginger, beets, burdock, lotus root, sweet potatoes and yams. Also closely related are carrots, celery, celeriac, parsley and fennel.

BULBS

Known for their ability to dissolve fats and excess mucus, bulbs are particularly heart healthy. Additionally, garlic's anti-inflammatory, antibacterial and antiviral properties make it a powerful healer. Look for garlic, leeks, onions, scallions and shallots.

SQUASH

With both winter and summer varieties, you can benefit year round from the blood-alkalinizing properties of squash. I am a fan of winter squash, which contain significant amounts of carbohydrates and sugars as well as vitamin A. My favorites include acorn, butternut, kabocha, dumpling, pumpkin, buttercup, delicata, red kuri and hubbard.

HERBS

The variety of herbs on the market today warrants a separate cookbook! Herbs can heal the sick, cleanse the blood and uplift the spirit, not to mention their ability to enhance your food and delight your palate. Experiment freely with fresh herbs in the summer and dried in the winter. Keep a bouquet handy on your countertop to snip into your cooking, and don't be afraid to spice up your food and your life.

SEA VEGETABLES

The health benefits of these gems from the sea are so outstanding that you really must give them a try! Sea vegetables offer a super-rich and easily absorbable source of minerals and vitamins, including iron, calcium, vitamin B, vitamin A, potassium, magnesium, phosphorus, iodine, zinc, selenium and copper. Sea vegetables, which are highly alkaline forming, help to reduce tumors and masses and bind to radioactive substances and heavy metals to pull them from our bodies. The most widely available include wakame, kombu (kelp), nori, arame and dulse.

There are simply far too many vegetable varieties to cover them all, but some of my other favorites include shiitake, portobello and cremini mushrooms, artichokes, asparagus, avocados, corn, cucumbers, endive, escarole, green beans, jícama, peas, frisée and heirloom tomatoes.

TAKE THE VEGETABLE CHALLENGE!

Try one new vegetable every week. At the end of a year you're likely to have a new vocabulary of vegetables and a whole new repertoire of recipes.

LEGUMES/BEANS

Legumes offer a host of health benefits that make them a highly sought after, nonanimal source of protein. While legumes, like grains, contain phytic acid *(see page 21)*, it is easily neutralized by soaking before cooking. Doing so yields an easily digestible source of protein that is rich in absorbable nutrients, supports thyroid function, balances blood sugar levels and regulates hormone activity.

A close look at legumes brings up frequently asked questions about protein – what is it and why is it so important? Popular weight loss diets have brought much attention to protein, but not always enough understanding. It's time to set the record straight: Proteins are building blocks – the stuff that allows babies to grow, young children to thrive and athletes to gain strength. The average adult requires approximately 10 percent of their diet to consist of protein. Pregnant and nursing mothers, young children, athletes and the elderly often require more.

Protein becomes a problem when it is consumed in excess, and even more so when it is largely animal based. In short, excess protein causes constipation, interferes with the absorption of calcium and minerals, and can cause serious illness over time, including weakening and even permanently damaging the liver and kidneys. Adding to these issues, a diet heavy in animal protein increases the risk of heart disease, elevated blood pressure and certain forms of cancer. Legumes are not linked to these health risks.

If you have kept away from legumes due to their negative side effects, start with the smaller varieties and follow the cooking instructions on the next page. To help reduce gas, pre-soak, rinse and skim away foam that develops during cooking. Kombu (the same sea vegetable we add to grains to increase their alkalinity) can also be added to legumes during cooking to decrease their gaseousness, to tenderize them and to provide added nutrients such as calcium, iron, B vitamins and trace minerals.

LEGUMES

Aduki beans*	Kidney beans
Black beans	Lentils*
Black-eyed peas	Mung beans*
Black soybeans	Pinto beans
Chickpeas (Garbanzo beans)	Red beans
Great northern beans	Soybeans
	Split peas

*no presoaking required

While there is no replacement for freshly cooked legumes, I do find it helpful to keep cans of prepared legumes in my pantry for last-minute or quick meals. One company in particular – Eden – offers prepared organic beans made with kombu. When using canned beans, a 30-second soak in boiling water followed by a cold rinse is a great way to freshen them up.

LEGUMES – BASIC COOKING INSTRUCTIONS

Don't be afraid to make large quantities, as extra legumes can be stored in an airtight container in the freezer. Most dried beans cook as follows:

1 cup dried beans of choice
  (yields 2¼ cups cooked beans)
Water
Thumb-size piece kombu
Pinch of sea salt

Sort through dry legumes and remove any dirt chunks and pebbles. Place legumes in pot with 3 cups water and soak overnight. Drain, rinse and return to pot with 3 cups fresh water. Cover pot, bring to boil, skim off foam and reduce heat to simmer. Add kombu and salt. Cover and cook until beans are tender (about 50 minutes). Drain remaining liquid and store cooked legumes in an airtight container in the refrigerator or freezer.

SOY

Soy falls into the legume family, but because there is so much confusion about whether soy is healthy or not, it warrants its own section. The United States produces and exports a vast amount of soy. Unfortunately, much of the soy grown in the U.S. is genetically engineered, riddled with herbicides and pesticides, unlabeled as such, and widely used in processed foods. Unless the package reads "USDA Organic" there is no way to be sure you are getting quality soy.

There is much contradictory information circulating about the health benefits and health risks of soy. Many people believe that soy products can be helpful in replacing estrogen for women, regulating thyroid and hormonal function, lowering blood cholesterol and fighting cancer. I cannot say for sure whether these claims are true, but this is what I do know:

The protein makeup of soy is particularly hard to digest and assimilate. It is high in phytic acid, which prevents our bodies from absorbing essential minerals such as calcium and iron (see page 21). Soybeans also contain goitrogens (found in foods such as cabbage and cauliflower), which interfere with thyroid function by suppressing the body's use of iodine.

It is, however, widely believed that slow cooking and fermenting soy neutralizes its high acid levels, allowing us to access its health benefits with less concern over its health risks. Therefore, when it comes to managing soy intake, you can eliminate many of these concerns by sticking with organic, fermented or slowly cooked soy products prepared with kombu and consumed in medicinal quantities based on your unique constitution.

FERMENTED AND/OR SLOW-COOKED SOY PRODUCTS

Miso	Tamari/Shoyu
Tempeh	Tofu

Of concern is the fact that non-nutritive soy in the form of highly processed isolated soy protein is used extensively in processed and packaged foods. At its core, isolated soy protein is the waste by-product of processed soy. And, like many processed preservatives, sweeteners, and emulsifiers, these additives have little nutritional value and pose significant health risks.

Soy is so overused in processed foods that it is nearly impossible to avoid unless you adhere to a strictly whole-food-based diet. It seems that every other label I read lists soy in one form or another. There are soy substitutes for many of the products we've elected to reduce or eliminate from our diets: soy cheese, soy milk, soy yogurt, soy nuts, soy hotdogs, soy butter, soy everything! The result? Excessive amounts of overprocessed soy in the American diet, causing a great deal of imbalance and disease. This is a good reason to stick with quality organic soy and reduce or even eliminate processed foods.

NUTS AND SEEDS

We now understand that protein inhibits the body from absorbing calcium. This presents a major problem for those of us who like to combine rice, beans and greens (and maybe even some pumpkin seeds or sesame seeds sprinkled on top). In a perfect world, we would eat each food group separately for maximum absorption and minimum stress on the body and digestive system. However, that perfect world would also be quite bland! Eaten separately, nuts and seeds offer protein and fat, which convert to energy without the worry of negating calcium and mineral absorption. This makes nuts and seeds perfect snack foods.

However, not all nuts and seeds are created equal. Almonds, walnuts, pistachios, cashews and pecans offer beneficial and essential fats linked to decreased risk of heart disease. But nuts such as pine nuts, Brazil nuts and hazelnuts are full of saturated fats which can contribute to heart disease. They are difficult for the body to break down and should be eaten less frequently. Seeds, on the other hand, offer similar beneficial fats as nuts plus a host of healing properties, vitamins and minerals. Try pumpkin seeds for added zinc, sesame seeds for calcium and flax seeds for essential fatty acids and lignans (cancer-fighting compounds).

RECOMMENDED NUTS AND SEEDS

Almonds	Pistachios
Cashews	Pumpkin seeds
Flax seeds (must be ground)	Sesame seeds
	Sunflower seeds
Pecans	Walnuts

If you've noticed the absence of peanuts from this list, it is because they are actually a legume, not a nut. Peanuts are a high-allergen food, have a high mold content and tend to be grown with significant amounts of pesticides. Organic peanuts however, can be a great source of protein and fat if these other factors are not an issue for you.

To prevent nuts and seeds from becoming rancid, store them in a cool, dark place and buy only as much as you will use in a short period of time. Nuts and seeds become rancid more readily when they are shelled or hulled. Refrigeration helps maintain freshness longer.

BASIC COOKING INSTRUCTIONS

PAN-ROASTING SEEDS
Place skillet over low heat and add seeds. Stir continuously until seeds become fragrant and start to brown. Remove from heat, cool completely and store in airtight container.

OVEN-ROASTING NUTS OR SEEDS
Preheat oven to 300°F. Place nuts or seeds on parchment-lined cookie sheet. Place in oven and roast — 10 minutes for seeds and 20 minutes for nuts, gently tossing every 5 minutes to prevent burning. When lightly browned and fragrant, remove from oven and lift parchment paper with nuts or seeds off cookie sheet to prevent continued roasting. Cool completely and store in airtight container.

OILS

Nut and seed oils offer beneficial fats and health benefits similar to those of whole nuts and seeds, but pay attention to how the oils are processed, packaged and stored. All nut and seed oils will break down under high heat, in the refining process and even from exposure to light. This makes it essential to buy cold-pressed, unrefined oils. Look for brands that package their oils in tinted glass bottles or cans, to reduce harmful exposure to light as well as contamination from plastic bottles.

When purchasing olive oil, I always select unrefined extra virgin which comes from the first press and is never heated or exposed to chemical processing. Darker oils often have a more intense olive flavor, but color is also influenced by the region and growing conditions of the olives, so don't rely on color to determine if a particular oil is less processed or refined. Read labels carefully to make sure you are getting first press, unrefined oil, and experiment with different brands to find the right balance of bitterness, smoothness and aroma to please your palate.

For cooking, I recommend either extra virgin olive oil or grapeseed oil. These two oils have the highest burn thresholds (grapeseed oil being the highest) and can better withstand the heat of a sauté pan without breaking down and becoming rancid and toxic. I often do what I call a water sauté, where I start with a small amount of oil and then add water to achieve a sautéed texture without the negative health effects of the heated oil. Additional high-quality oil can be added after cooking to infuse dishes with more flavor and health benefits.

Toasted sesame oil is highly sensitive to heat and should not be used for frying. This aromatic oil can be added in small quantities to dishes after cooking to give exceptional flavor and aroma.

RECOMMENDED OILS

Unrefined cold-pressed extra virgin olive oil

Unrefined grapeseed oil

Cold pressed toasted sesame oil

With the exception of olive and grapeseed oils, all nut and seed oils should be stored in the refrigerator to prevent them from becoming rancid.

FRUIT

Rarely do people need help incorporating more fruit into their diets. Few can resist biting into a crisp apple or juicy pear in the fall, picking fresh berries or snacking on melon in the summer and enjoying oranges and grapefruits in the winter. In fact, even once-obscure fruits like pomegranates and mangoes have made their way into our diets with regularity.

Fruit offers a variety of health benefits, ranging from the soluble fiber of apples and pears to the ellagic acid (an anticancer compound) and antioxidants found in berries. But the high sugar content of fresh and dried fruit makes overindulgence – particularly in juice – a significant problem. If you are a juice drinker and you'd like to get a sense of how much fruit you consume in a day, you can either take out your vegetable juicer or make a trip to your local juice bar. The goal is to observe exactly how much fruit it takes to make a small glass of juice. You may be surprised to learn that your morning glass of juice likely contains all, if not more than, your daily fruit allowance.

When it comes to quantity, the only person who understands how your body reacts to fruit, sugar or any other food group for that matter, is *you*.

Remember, sweet is one of the essential five tastes. If we don't include it in our diets in a nutritional form, then we will be more likely to crave it nonnutritionally. The challenge is to find the sweet that best suits your delicate balance. While sweeteners may be part of your sweetness mix, you'll seldom go wrong with whole fruits and vegetables.

MINIMALLY PROCESSED SWEETENERS

Agave nectar	Maple syrup
Barley malt	Molasses
Brown rice syrup	Stevia
Honey (not vegetarian)	

See "What's That?" *(beginning page 27)* for more information on individual sweeteners and refined sugar.

Notes About Oxalic and Phytic Acids

You may notice that certain vegetables are featured much more than others in this book. Some vegetables contain oxalic acid, which makes their nutrients difficult to assimilate and can even pull important minerals such as calcium from the bones. Consumed regularly, this acid can lead to irritation of the digestive system, stomach and kidneys. For most people, it is unnecessary to eliminate these vegetables. But, if you have a family history or are concerned about arthritis, osteoporosis or mineral absorption in general, you may want to limit your intake of these vegetables in favor of the vegetables mentioned on page 15.

VEGETABLES HIGH IN OXALIC ACID

Beets and beet greens	Rhubarb
Bell peppers	Sorrel
Chives	Spinach
Parsley	Swiss chard

OTHER FOODS CONTAINING OXALIC ACID

Chocolate	Cranberries
Cocoa	Peanuts
Coffee	Strawberries

Another nonnutritional component, phytic acid, is found in grains, legumes and seeds. This acid binds to minerals and proteins and decreases the body's ability to absorb and utilize these nutrients. The earlier sections on these foods offer ways to eliminate or neutralize the phytic acid in them.

As you will notice, I limit the use of vegetables high in oxalic acid, and I regularly employ cooking techniques like presoaking grains and legumes to neutralize phytic acid and yield nutrients that are easier to assimilate and digest. These foods offer plenty of nutritional value and can even strengthen and heal certain constitutions, but they are not what I consider to be my daily heavy hitters. I use them for variety, but in much smaller quantities and with less frequency.

Remember, only you can feel your body's response to individual foods. This insight is provided to increase your knowledge and help you make healthy choices, but your unique in-house nutritionist – you – can best determine the right dietary mix for you. In the end, there's more to know and understand about nutrition than can be studied in a lifetime. Knowledge can empower us to make healthy choices, but it should be combined with a healthy dose of perspective so that it does not keep you from enjoying food for food's sake. Moderation, not deprivation, is key. Focus on filling your plate with the foods that heal you. Slowly, the foods that harm you will fall by the wayside.

Organic vs. Conventional

Only you can assess the importance of eating organic food for yourself and your family. In order to make that choice, it's important to understand exactly what organic means. Perhaps the greatest misperception is that organic refers to a particular variety of food. In fact, it refers to the way in which food is grown and produced. Organic foods are grown without the use of pesticides, herbicides, synthetic fertilizers and genetically modified organisms. Organic meats, fish, poultry, dairy and eggs all come from animals that have been raised free of growth hormones and antibiotics. This standard is regulated by the USDA National Organic Program.

Even knowing that, questions still arise. I hear the argument over and over, "My grandparents didn't eat organic and they lived to the ripe old age of … so why should I?" Excellent question. Here are some answers:

1. Their food supply was not as adulterated as ours is today and likely did not travel as far or as long to get from the farm to the grocery store to the table.

2. They did not eat processed or fast foods. Their meals were balanced and prepared fresh daily.

3. Fields were not sprayed with herbicides and pesticides to the extent that they had to be unfarmed for entire growing seasons in order to rest and be brought back to life.

4. Animals and fish were not fed steroids, growth hormones, antibiotics and pesticide-laden foods.

5. Produce was not genetically engineered or grown with pesticides so that it could be harvested at reduced cost and increase productivity; nor was it picked and then shipped across the country, tossed around in cases, placed on grocery shelves and intended to appear unblemished and freshly picked weeks later.

This topic warrants a separate book, and many have been written, but for our purposes it is important to simply clarify that **organic foods retain greater nutritional value and health benefits than the same foods grown conventionally.** That does not mean that everything in your kitchen must be organic. But it is a good reason to get to know your local farmer, to ask what has and has not been sprayed, to look for "ecologically grown" fruits and vegetables that are sprayed only if and when needed, to buy seasonal produce instead of tropical fruits or foods from other countries whose organic standards may vary from ours, and to be as aware of your food sources as possible.

The fruits and vegetables listed below tend to be grown with the highest and lowest levels of pesticides. Use this information to help evaluate your options and make healthy choices. These two lists were compiled by the Environmental Working Group.

All vegetables and fruits were washed (or peeled, when appropriate) before testing.

For more information on this and other health-related topics, visit www.ewg.org.

VEGETABLES AND FRUITS CONTAINING THE **HIGHEST** LEVEL OF PESTICIDES

Apples	Cherries	Nectarines	Potatoes
Bell peppers	Grapes (imported)	Peaches	Spinach
Celery	Lettuce	Pears	Strawberries

VEGETABLES AND FRUITS CONTAINING THE **LOWEST** LEVEL OF PESTICIDES

Asparagus	Broccoli	Eggplant	Onions
Avocados	Cabbage	Kiwis	Peas
Bananas	Corn	Mangoes	Pineapple

The following foods did not make it onto Environmental Working Group's top 12 list, but also tend to be grown with high levels of pesticides: winter squash, Mexican cantaloupe, green beans, apricots, soybeans, tomatoes, carrots, oranges, rice, tropical fruits, imported produce in general, almonds, sunflower seeds, peanuts and wheat.

When comparing organic to conventional, it is important to understand that organic standards in the United States differ from those abroad. Fruits and vegetables that are regularly sourced from out of the country may be exposed to farming practices that would not meet U.S. standards.

Additionally, many of the foods grown with high levels of pesticides (such as soy and wheat) are the very foods fed to the animals we consume. Combined with the common practice of animal farming with hormones and antibiotics, this makes a compelling case for purchasing organic dairy and meat products over conventional.

There is simply no denying – the cleaner the food, the healthier you.

Guide to Reading Recipes

I am a self-taught cook with a passion for preparing healthy foods that nurture and nourish my family and friends. My greatest cooking teacher, my mother, taught me that if I put good ingredients in, I am bound to get good results. These sage words have stuck with me over many years of experimenting and developing recipes. Sometimes the results are great – other times not so great! In those not-so-great instances, I often add the word *surprise* to the end of the recipe name. A failed Key lime pie, for instance, would kindly become Key Lime Surprise. Or in my mother's case, when we needed a spoon rather than a fork to enjoy it, it was dubbed "Key Lime Extravaganza"!

For me, the pursuit of wholesome, organic foods is every bit as much fun as the preparation. I love to talk to farmers about what's growing well, what they're enjoying the most and how they're preparing it. There is nothing more delicious than produce grown with respect and care, as opposed to the "empty" produce that travels across the country and is featured in many grocery stores.

WASHING INGREDIENTS

When we eat food from the earth with as little processing as possible, it is natural for some of the earth to get mixed in with it – whether we buy it at the farm, off the produce shelf or from a bulk bin. It is a good idea to wash all whole grains, vegetables, legumes, fruits and sea vegetables. Unless stated otherwise, these are the methods I use.

To clean whole grains and legumes, place them in a bowl and remove any unhulled grains, pieces of grass, pebbles and chunks of dirt. Fill the bowl with water, swish it around and pour off the water and anything that floats to the surface. Repeat until the water is clean.

Most fruits and vegetables that are not peeled can be washed in salt water. This method is particularly good for leafy greens and sprouts. Fill a bowl with enough water to cover vegetables, add 2–3 tablespoons salt, swish it around, remove greens, discard the water and repeat as needed. Sometimes leafy greens require an additional check and rinse.

Leeks tend to accumulate dirt between their layers. To clean, chop off the root end, slice in half lengthwise to fan the leek open, hold it under the faucet and rinse. Chop leeks across until you reach the dark outermost layer. Peel off that layer, rinse and continue chopping. Repeat to chop all light green layers (the dark outer layers are tough).

Sea vegetables, like legumes, can have dirt and other undesirable particles mixed in with them. Place them in a bowl, cover with water, swish around, drain and repeat until the water is clear.

MEASURING INGREDIENTS

I cook with my senses and hope this book empowers you to do the same. I rarely measure (except in testing these recipes) and my favorite cooking technique is "dump and stir." Whether you measure or not, your recipes are likely to come out different each time for a variety of reasons. Some vegetables (particularly dark leafy greens) will retain more water or less, which can alter the quantity once cooked. Your taste and texture preference may differ from mine, so feel free to adjust your outcome by increasing or decreasing the liquid, spice or any other ingredient. Finally, if you are drawn to a recipe but do not have all the ingredients, by all means, adapt the recipe accordingly.

COMMONLY USED INGREDIENTS

I purchase nearly all my Clean Food ingredients at either my local organic farm, a natural foods store or a conventional grocery store. Hard-to-find products are often easy to find online by conducting a simple search either by brand or product.

MISO

Miso is a living food that gives recipes a salty, rich flavor. The darker the miso, the longer it has been fermented and the stronger the flavor. Good quality living miso will be in your store's refrigerated section. Look for brands that use glass containers, as miso is a fermented food and is adversely affected by plastic. Powdered miso lacks the health benefits of the refrigerated paste. Never bring miso to a boil as doing so destroys its living enzymes. Experiment with different brands and types to discover the ones you like best.

OLIVE OIL

Read labels carefully to be sure you are getting first press, unrefined olive oil, and experiment with brands to find the right balance of bitterness, smoothness and aroma to please your senses.

PARSLEY

I use flat leaf parsley, also referred to as Italian parsley. While curly parsley can be substituted, I prefer the stronger flavor of flat leaf.

SALT

Look for sea salt, which contains more minerals than conventional table salt. When salt is listed as an ingredient it means fine salt unless coarse is specified. A good rule of thumb is, the grayer the salt, the less refined and the healthier.

TOASTED SESAME OIL

Use cold pressed oil. Hot sesame oil can be substituted as desired.

TAMARI, SHOYU AND BRAGG LIQUID AMINOS

These condiments can be used interchangeably according to your preference and health requirements. Tamari and shoyu are fermented, but Bragg's is not. For more information about the differences between the three, refer to "What's That" *(pages 28, 33, and 34).*

VEGAN MAYONNAISE

Vegan mayonnaise is available at nearly all grocery stores. My favorite – Grapeseed Oil Vegenaise by Follow Your Heart – is found in the refrigerated section of the store.

TOFU

To guarantee quality, look for brands that use organic soy and nigari, as opposed to calcium chloride, as a natural coagulating agent and be sure to check freshness dates. Store opened tofu for up to three days in the refrigerator in a container with water to cover and change the water daily. To make tofu easier to digest, steam it for 10 minutes before using.

VEGETABLE STOCK

Vegetable stock can be purchased in powder form or prepared and packaged in cartons. The infused water that remains from reconstituting dried shiitake mushrooms or sun-dried tomatoes makes a delicious stock, as does leftover water from steaming or boiling vegetables.

When it comes to Clean Food, what you see is what you get, but that doesn't mean you'll automatically know what it is! With more than 100 cooking classes under my belt, the most commonly asked question, hands down, is, "What's that?" From aduki beans and agar to wakame and wasabi, there's intention behind each ingredient. The more we understand about our food, the greater healing power we have and the more equipped and inspired we can be to add nutritional punch to all of our cooking. So fill your kitchen with foods that don't require labels, labeled foods with only natural ingredients — as few as possible and nothing else — and enjoy how delicious good health can be.

ADUKI BEAN
A legume, tangy in flavor, easy to digest and known to benefit the kidneys and detoxify the body. Pairs well with sweet winter squash and root vegetables.

AGAR
Sea vegetable known for its gelling ability and high mineral content *(see Sea Vegetables)*.

AGAVE NECTAR
Natural sweetener derived from cactus, low in sucrose and with a low glycemic index, making it safe for diabetics.

ALMONDS
High in monosaturated fats thought to help fight heart disease by lowering cholesterol. A rich source of magnesium and the antioxidant vitamin E.

AMARANTH
High protein, non-gluten grain high in fiber, calcium, lysine and vitamins. Has a nutty flavor that mixes well with other grains, thickens soups and helps retain moisture when used for baking.

APPLE CIDER VINEGAR
Imparts a warming, sour and bitter flavor to food. As a home remedy, it can be helpful for everything from sore throats and digestive issues to elevated blood pressure, sinus problems and weight loss.

ARAME
Sea vegetable with a very mild taste. Needs only to be soaked, not boiled, before eating (making it an easy addition to salads and grain dishes). A good place to start if you're new to cooking with sea vegetables *(see Sea Vegetables)*.

ARROWROOT
Natural thickening agent made from a tropical root. Comes in powdered form and is used as a more nutritious substitute for cornstarch.

ASIAN GREENS
Members of the cabbage family with a mild taste. Can be eaten raw in salad, or cooked in stir fry or noodle dishes. Includes bok choy, pac choy, tatsoi, Napa cabbage and Chinese broccoli.

ASPARAGUS
Particularly high in folate, which helps prevent birth defects if consumed in the first trimester of pregnancy. Supports cardiovascular health, and is a natural diuretic.

AVOCADO
An excellent source of the monosaturated fatty acids that protect against elevated cholesterol, blood pressure and even some forms of cancer.

BAKING POWDER
Look for brands that are aluminum- and gluten-free, like Rumford or Featherweight.

BALSAMIC VINEGAR
Traditional Italian vinegar made from the juice of grapes. It is fermented and aged and has a sweet, rich and woody taste.

BARLEY
Whole hulled barley has significantly greater nutritional value than pearl barley and is known for its ability to soothe digestion and heal and strengthen the liver, spleen, pancreas and intestines. Barley's taste is nutty and chewy.

BARLEY MALT
Naturally processed, low-sucrose grain sweetener derived from whole barley.

BLACK BEANS
Also known as black turtle beans, a high-protein legume beneficial to the kidneys and liver. Can help relieve symptoms of menopause.

BRAGG LIQUID AMINOS
Condiment that tastes like soy sauce with a hint of maple. Provides essential building blocks of complete protein.

BROWN RICE
Some believe that rice is the most balanced food. It is full of vitamins, minerals, fiber, complex carbohydrates and protein and is especially high in B vitamins, calcium, phosphorous, vitamin E and iron. Brown rice can bring the body into a deep state of balance. Popular varieties include short grain, long grain, medium grain (golden rose) and basmati.

BROWN RICE SYRUP
Naturally processed sweetener derived from fermented brown rice and less destructive to our natural mineral balance than refined sweeteners. It is 50 percent maltose (unlike white, brown and raw sugars, which are 96+ percent sucrose, and maple syrup, which is 65 percent sucrose). When substituting, use 1½ cups of brown rice syrup per cup of sugar and adjust dry ingredients as appropriate to achieve desired texture.

BROWN RICE VINEGAR
Imparts a sweet flavor and is commonly used in Asian cooking. Its warming nature helps stimulate circulation and remove stagnation from the body.

BURDOCK
Root vegetable that cleanses the blood and strengthens the intestines. Highly alkalinizing and helpful for reducing sweet cravings.

CANOLA OIL
A monosaturated oil from the rapeseed plant.

CHICKPEAS (Garbanzo Beans)
Legume high in protein, fiber and iron. They help lower cholesterol, regulate blood sugar and increase energy.

CINNAMON
A warming spice helpful for reducing risk of heart disease, fighting systemic yeast (candida), regulating blood sugar and relieveing flu and cold symptoms.

COCONUT MILK
Recent research shows coconut milk to be a healthy source of fat, but I am still leery of its impact on cardiovascular health. Coconut milk has a sweet taste and a warming effect in the body. It is a complete protein and is often used as a substitute for oil.

COLLARD GREENS
These greens are nutritional heavy hitters! A rich source of calcium, manganese, chlorophyll, antioxidant vitamins A and C, minerals, cancer-fighting phytonutrients and much more. They provide strong immune support and protect, cleanse and nourish the heart, liver, colon, lungs and the cellular system in general.

CUMIN
A pungent spice that helps circulation, energy and metabolism and pairs well with legumes, winter squash and whole grains.

DAIKON

This Japanese radish tastes milder than red radishes, breaks down mucus (particularly in the lungs) and is excellent for lowering cholesterol.

DANDELION GREENS

Bitter by nature, these super cleansers are rich in purifying chlorophyll and helpful for reestablishing healthy intestinal flora. Dried dandelions are used medicinally in teas, as a diuretic, to strengthen the liver and to promote healthy digestion and circulation.

EDAMAME

Fresh soybeans that are boiled in their pods and served with salt.

EGG REPLACER

There are many options for replacing eggs in recipes. The one you select depends on what you want the eggs to accomplish. Sometimes eggs are used to bind ingredients, sometimes as a leavening agent, sometimes for moisture. Common substitutes include applesauce or ground flax seeds. To replace one egg using flax, combine 1 tablespoon ground golden flax seed with 3 tablespoons water. Let sit 10 minutes, then add to recipe. The easiest and most dependable egg replacer is a powdered mix by Ener-G Foods that can be found in most natural food stores.

FENNEL

A soothing vegetable from the parsley family that tastes like licorice or anise. Medicinally, fennel is thought to calm intestinal and stomach cramps, gas and stomach pain. It also contains phytoestrogens helpful during menopause.

FERMENTED BLACK BEANS

Used traditionally in Chinese and Thai cuisine, these small black beans are fermented and preserved in salt. Available in Asian food stores or in the Asian food section of natural food stores.

FLAX SEEDS

The richest source of omega-3 fatty acids, flax seeds cleanse the heart and arteries, provide immune strength and support liver function. The body cannot break down flax seeds in their whole form so be sure to grind them into a meal before using. Flax oil, the processed by-product of flax seeds, can be purchased in liquid or capsule form. Unlike the seed, the oil should not be consumed by men, as it has been positively linked with enlarged prostate.

GALANGAL

Closely related to ginger, but with a more yellow translucent skin and a peppery, citrus taste. Available in Asian food stores.

GARLIC

A powerful healer with a warming, sweet and pungent taste. Offers many health benefits including cardiovascular support. It has anti-inflammatory, antibacterial and antiviral properties, as well as cancer-fighting phytonutrients.

GINGER

A pungent, warming spice that helps alleviate inflammation and gastrointestinal upset, promotes circulation and digestion, strengthens immunity and fights cancer.

GOMASIO

Macrobiotic condiment made of ground toasted sesame seeds and sea salt.

GRAPESEED OIL

Excellent for cooking. Withstands high temperatures without breaking down, and is heart healthy.

HIJIKI

Recent studies have found hijiki to contain high levels of arsenic, making this one sea vegetable to avoid.

HONEY

Non-vegetarian, unprocessed sweetener highly regarded as a healer. When consumed raw, honey acts as an antibacterial, antiviral and antifungal agent. Athletes find honey to be a pure source of the energy, carbohydrates and glycogen needed to fuel and heal muscle tissue. Local honey can be helpful for treating seasonal allergies.

JÍCAMA

This root looks like a turnip, but tastes like a cross between an apple, pear and potato. Peel away and discard its fibrous skin and use the white flesh raw in Mexican dishes or with crudités. Cooked, jícama takes on the flavor of the other ingredients used.

KAFFIR LIME

Citrus leaves traditionally used in Thai cooking. Can be minced and added to soups and sauces or added whole and removed before serving.

KALE

Offers a rich supply of vitamins A and C, calcium, fiber, phytonutrients and chlorophyll. A powerful detoxifier, healer and ally in fighting cancer, heart disease, cataracts, inflammation, arthritis and diseases of the colon.

KELP

An effective digestive aid that supports kidney and thyroid function. Helps balance hormones and is useful for breaking down hardened masses in the body. Powdered kelp, available in natural food stores, is easy to add to soups, sauces, batters and even smoothies for an added nutritional punch without a seaweed taste (*see* Sea Vegetables).

KIDNEY BEANS

Like most legumes, these are particularly helpful for regulating blood sugar and providing easily absorbable protein, fiber and iron. Health benefits include reducing cholesterol and the risk of heart attack, improving brain function and providing slow burning, long-lasting energy. If gas becomes a problem when consuming kidney beans, start with smaller varieties of legumes.

KOMBU

A small piece added to grains, soups, sauces and legumes during cooking is an easy way to infuse foods with highly alkalinizing minerals, iodine and iron. Dried kombu reconstitutes and releases its nutrients into the cooking liquid that is then absorbed by your food. Also known for its ability to tenderize legumes and reduce their gaseous properties (*see* Sea Vegetables).

KUDZU (KUZU)

Japanese tuber that has a cooling and soothing effect on the stomach. Kudzu is most frequently found in powdered form and is a healthy and easy thickening agent. Substitute 1:1 for cornstarch.

LEEK

Offers many of the same health benefits as garlic and onions, but is much milder and sweeter than these other powerhouse vegetables. Leeks are also excellent blood sugar stabilizers and blood pressure regulators. They look like huge scallions.

LEMONGRASS

An aromatic herb used in Thai cuisine that imparts a light citrus flavor and bouquet. Commonly used to flavor soups.

LENTILS

Share many of the same health benefits of other legumes, but particularly high in iron.

MAPLE SYRUP

Known as liquid gold in my home, this naturally processed sweetener from maple trees is only 65 percent sucrose and much less destructive to the body's natural mineral balance than processed sweeteners like white, brown or raw sugar. When substituting for white sugar, use 1¼ cups maple syrup per cup of sugar.

MILLET

Sweet, nutty grain that combines well with sweet winter squash and root vegetables. Has a settling effect on the stomach and is healing to the spleen and pancreas. Because millet is naturally alkalinizing, it is not necessary to cook it with kombu.

MIRIN

Sweet Japanese cooking wine made from fermented brown rice, rice koji for fermenting, water and salt. Avoid brands with added corn syrup or alcohol.

MISO

Most commonly made from fermented soy beans, this paste comes in many varieties, offering different tastes and colors. Contains living enzymes that aid digestion and help maintain healthy intestinal flora. Miso is a rich source of minerals. It tones and cleanses the body of toxins and metals such as radiation and mercury, and it helps the body assimilate good cholesterol and break down the bad. For non-soy varieties, look for chickpea, aduki bean and sweet brown rice miso.

MOCHI

Made from pressed sweet brown rice, mochi is easy to digest, warming and strengthening. To use, cut blocks into squares, bake and serve plain or with filling.

MUNG BEANS

Highly cooling legumes thought to aid the liver and gallbladder and to cleanse the cardiovascular system. Can be eaten cooked or sprouted.

MUSTARD GREENS

Greens with a pungent and peppery taste. Can be eaten raw or cooked. Help break down and cleanse the body of mucus, prevent cancer, provide absorbable calcium and phytonutrients, promote heart and lung health, fight inflammation and even help reduce hot flashes during menopause.

NORI

Similar benefits to those of kelp. Has the highest mineral content of all sea vegetables. Particularly helpful for lowering cholesterol and blood pressure and for breaking down and flushing away cysts and mucus.

OATS (Whole Oat Groats)

Powerhouse of a grain most noted for its ability to flush cholesterol from the arteries. Incredibly soothing, healing and restorative to the reproductive, nervous and digestive systems. Provides abundant antioxidants and lignans, which protect against cancer and help stabilize blood sugar levels. Rolled oats, which are only minimally processed, are slightly less beneficial than steel cut or whole oat groats.

OLIVE OIL

A rich source of polyphenols and essential fats that lubricate organs, cleanse and support nearly every bodily system. Look for cold pressed extra virgin varieties for maximum health benefits.

PARCEL

A leafy herb that looks much like parsley and tastes like celery. A great addition to soups and salads without the bulk of a stalk.

PARSLEY

High in antioxidants and vitamins C and A, this blood purifier makes a great condiment on whole grains, legumes, vegetables, tofu, chicken and fish. Bring it home, wash it in salty water, pat it dry and arrange it in a vase on your counter so you remember to use a bit each day.

PARSNIP

This sweet root vegetable is a winter favorite and becomes sweeter in frosty weather. Parsnips look like white carrots. They are particularly healing to the stomach and cleansing to the liver and gallbladder.

PICKLED GINGER

Pickles aid digestion. Add to that ginger's stomach-calming ability and great flavor, and you've got a great healing combination.

PINTO BEANS

Like other legumes, these are high in fiber and protein, stabilize blood sugar and lower cholesterol. A rich source of vitamin B1, iron, magnesium, copper and potassium.

PISTACHIO NUTS

A great source of protein, vitamin E and antioxidants, and beneficial to the liver, kidneys and heart.

POMEGRANATE

Thought to have mystical powers, the edible seeds of this ancient fruit are cleansing and cooling. They benefit the cardiovascular system and help stabilize blood sugar. For more juice, select larger fruit with reddish brown firm skin.

PUMPKIN SEEDS

Also known as pepitas, these seeds are a rich source of zinc, iron, and omega-3 fatty acids. They support immune strength and offer essential monosaturated fats and protein.

QUINOA

High protein, non-gluten grain from the Incas. It is a complete protein with significant amounts of lysine, helpful for repairing tissue. Like other whole grains, quinoa helps fight cancer, prevents heart disease and lowers the risk of type 2 diabetes. Has a slightly bitter taste that pairs well with dark leafy greens like collards and kale, sweet root vegetables, corn and onions.

REFINED SUGAR

I call this filler food because it sneaks into your diet and takes the place of foods that can strengthen, nourish and heal you. Refined sugar negatively affects the nervous system, kidney function, mood and nutrient absorption. It is linked to imbalances in the body and brain as well as the depletion of nutrients necessary for healthy metabolism.

RUTABAGA

Sweet, strengthening and warming root vegetable that lends itself well to roasting, puréeing or adding to soups and stews. Often dipped in wax to preserve over the winter. Look for firm, smooth and unblemished skin.

SEA SALT

Conventional table salt is highly processed, nutritionally empty and can pose health risks. Sea salt (usually slightly gray in color), on the other hand, is minimally processed, retains much of its natural mineral content and is highly alkalinizing. Sea salt has many benefits, including neutralizing acidity, tenderizing and enhancing flavors.

SEA VEGETABLES

No other foods offer such a rich supply of minerals. They also provide significant amounts of iodine, iron, calcium, magnesium, B vitamins and lignans (cancer-fighting compounds). Used medicinally to prevent and fight cancer, regulate the thyroid, promote heart health, relieve symptoms of menopause and reduce inflammation. For information on specific varieties, see Agar, Arame, Kelp, Kombu, Nori and Wakame.

SEITAN

High protein "wheat meat" made from wheat gluten.

SESAME OIL (Toasted)

When unrefined and cold pressed, it is monosaturated and a healthy source of essential fats. As with other quality oils, heating destroys its beneficial qualities and makes it toxic, so be sure to add sesame oil and other aromatic oils to food *after* cooking.

SESAME SEEDS

A rich source of calcium. Black sesame seeds have stronger medicinal value than lighter varieties.

SHIITAKE MUSHROOMS

A powerful healer and delicious addition to many dishes. They protect the body from cancer, decrease fat and cholesterol in the blood and flush the body of stagnating toxins. Dried shiitakes are stronger medicinally than fresh ones, and can be soaked in hot water to reconstitute. Use the soaking liquid as a healing stock for soups and teas.

SHOYU

Soy sauce made from soybeans, water, sea salt and wheat.

SUCANAT

Minimally processed sugar made by pressing the juice from the cane, clarifying, filtering and evaporating it, then crystallizing the resulting sugar. Sucanat retains many of the minerals, vitamins and trace elements found in sugar cane.

SUMMER SQUASH

Much more delicate than their winter counterparts, summer squash is cooling, refreshing and versatile. Try serving squash raw and shredded in salads, grilled, roasted or sautéed. Look for crookneck, straightneck, zucchini and pattypan varieties.

SUNFLOWER SEEDS

Warming in nature and a rich source of protein, vitamins D, B1 and E. For people with tree-nut allergies, try sunflower butter as a substitute for peanut or almond butters.

SUSHI RICE

Traditional Japanese short grain rice that grows white and pearl-like naturally. Lighter texture than brown rice. To make it less sticky and more manageable, brown rice vinegar and brown rice syrup are often added.

SWEET BROWN RICE

High in protein and good fats, easy to digest and more glutinous in texture than regular brown rice, although still gluten-free.

TAHINI

Rich and warming butter made from sesame seeds. Comes in both regular (slightly more bitter) and roasted varieties.

TAMARI

Soy sauce made from soybeans, water and sea salt. Traditionally wheat-free, but not all manufacturers follow this guideline. Has a high sodium content, but reduced sodium tamari is available at most natural food stores.

TAMARIND

Fruits from this tree are commonly used in Asian, Indian and Mexican cuisines. Tamarinds have a tangy sweet-and-sour taste and consist of a pit surrounded by a red flesh. They are similar in texture to dates.

TEFF (Ivory and Dark)

A high protein, non-gluten grain, high in iron, calcium and zinc. Because it is such a small grain, it is impossible to hull before milling, making teff flour nearly identical in nutritional value to the whole grain. Dark teff is higher in iron, while ivory teff is higher in protein.

TEMPEH

Made from pressed and fermented soybeans. Comes in many varieties based on added ingredients such as grains and vegetables. It is 19.5 percent protein, rich in unsaturated fat, and highly alkalinizing, strengthening and easy to digest.

TOFU

Made from soybean curd. Regular tofu holds its shape and texture, and silken is used for whipping in dressings and puddings. It is high in protein, calcium, B-vitamins, potassium and iron and low in saturated fat and sodium. Tofu is rich in isoflavones thought to reduce women's risk of breast cancer, and phytoestrogens which block harmful estrogens from being absorbed by the cells.

TOMATILLO

Also known as a husk tomato, tomatillos are commonly used in Mexican cuisine and add a crisp tartness to dishes. Look for fruits with brown husks and smooth green skin.

UDON/SOBA NOODLES

Wheat or buckwheat noodles commonly used in Asian cooking. Look for varieties made with wild yam and/or mung bean.

UMEBOSHI PLUMS

Quite sour and salty, these Japanese plums are pickled and used to aid digestion and help treat liver imbalances. Highly alkalinizing to the blood and antibiotic in nature. Similar health benefits can be gained from umeboshi paste and vinegar, but be mindful of sodium content.

WAKAME

Sea vegetable most commonly served in miso soup. Add a small amount of dried wakame to hot water and let steep 3–4 minutes before stirring in the desired amount of dissolved miso (*see* Sea Vegetables).

WALNUTS

Super-rich in omega 3 fatty acids, these nuts benefit the heart and brain and heal imbalances caused by inflammation. Also a rich source of ellagic acid, an antioxidant that boosts immune strength and helps prevent cancer.

WASABI

Spicy Japanese mustard usually made from horseradish root and often colored with spirulina. Look for paste or powdered varieties packaged without preservatives.

WATERCRESS

Slightly more pungent than other bitter greens. Effective blood purifier that helps remove toxins from the body. High in vitamin A, chlorophyll and calcium. Can be eaten cooked or raw. Mix with lettuce to amp up the nutritional value of your salad.

WATERMELON RADISH

This radish looks like a turnip and should be bought when smooth and firm. Peel and discard the fibrous skin to reveal a beautiful deep pink flesh. If you can't find watermelon radishes, substitute red radishes, jícama or even red pepper.

WHEAT BERRIES

The whole wheat grain. Comes in two varieties – hard, which has more gluten, and soft, which has less gluten but more starch. Can be cooked and used like rice in recipes. Has a nutty taste and requires much chewing power to ensure healthy digestion.

WILD RICE

Not a grain, but a water grass. Grows along streams and swamps and is high in protein and low in fat.

WINTER SQUASH

A rich source of vitamins A, C, B1, folate, fiber and omega-3 fatty acids, these gems of the fall are sweet, warming, easy to digest, helpful for improving circulation and are mood enhancing. Look for acorn, buttercup, butternut, delicata, hubbard, kabocha, pumpkin and red kuri.

Oh, give us pleasure in the flowers today;
And give us not to think so far away
As the uncertain harvest; keep us here
All simply in the springing of the year.

ROBERT FROST

Spring

The very sight of overflowing baskets of tender baby greens that adorn the organic farmers market each spring lifts my spirit and heals my soul. The kale and collard greens melt in your mouth and there are enough varieties of Chinese cabbage and lettuce greens to enjoy a new one each day. Spring's increased sunshine and longer days start a natural gentle cleansing that prepares me for warmer days ahead. As everything starts to blossom and temperatures rise, I feel a renewed sense of community, connection and hope. Each conversation at the farm has a recipe involved. I listen as I wander around baskets of tender asparagus, artichokes, pac choy, fennel, watermelon radishes and green beans. My basket fills with tastes and textures all begging to come home with me. Whether you are looking to lighten up, gain mental clarity, energize or simply take advantage of spring's delicious bounty, it's time to get cooking.

SPRING

Traditional Hummus

THIS IS THE PERFECT RECIPE to start this book. Hummus was the first dish I figured out on my own, and years later I still make it by the tubful. Whether stuffed in pita pockets with vegetables and sprouts, or served as an appetizer or midday snack with carrot sticks or rice crackers, hummus is easy to make, healthy and enjoyed by all. For variety, try adding roasted garlic or roasted red peppers.

1	garlic clove, peeled
2	cups cooked chickpeas
3	tablespoons extra virgin olive oil
2	tablespoons tahini
½	teaspoon ground cumin
2	tablespoons lemon juice
¼	teaspoon sea salt
Water	

With food processor running, drop in garlic clove and process until minced. Turn off processor, scrape down sides and add chickpeas, olive oil, tahini, cumin, lemon juice and salt. Restart processor and slowly add water, making hummus slightly thinner than desired, as it will thicken when refrigerated. Chill to combine flavors before serving.

MAKES 1½ cups

Muffaletto

THIS CONDIMENT WHIPS UP IN SECONDS and has many wonderful uses. Try it in a wrap with hummus and arugula, serve it as an appetizer with Pita Chips *(page 261)* or toasted baguette rounds, or thin it with a bit of wine and some chopped tomatoes and use it as a pasta sauce.

1   cup black and green olives, pitted
1   cup roasted red pepper
2   garlic cloves, peeled
¼ cup chopped fresh parsley
1   tablespoon red wine vinegar
Freshly ground black pepper
Extra virgin olive oil

Combine olives, roasted pepper, garlic, parsley and vinegar in food processor and pulse to chop ingredients. Be sure not to purée – chunks are good! Season to taste with pepper and drizzle with olive oil. Cover and refrigerate 3 hours. Before serving, stir and bring to room temperature.

MAKES 1¼ cups

Green Goddess Dip

WHEN I PUT DINNER ON THE TABLE, my children quickly fill up on the least nutritious part of the meal and then complain they're too full to eat their vegetables. This dip is my solution. I serve it as an appetizer with crudités – my children feel like they're getting a treat, and I succeed in filling their bottomless pits with vegetables. Everybody wins!

12 ounces extra firm silken tofu

3 scallions, chopped

3 tablespoons fresh parsley or cilantro

1 tablespoon maple mustard

Juice of 1 lemon

1 tablespoon brown rice vinegar

2 teaspoons mellow white miso

2 teaspoons brown rice syrup

3 tablespoons extra virgin olive oil

Water

Wrap tofu in paper towels and press gently to remove excess water. Place in food processor or blender and process until smooth. Add remaining ingredients and process to combine. Add water 1 tablespoon at a time to achieve desired consistency. Cover and refrigerate to thicken and allow flavors to blend. Store in airtight container in refrigerator for up to 3 days.

VARIATIONS

This dip can be thinned with water and used as a salad dressing, or made with 1½ cups great northern or navy beans instead of tofu.

MAKES 2 cups

Lemony Artichoke Dip

FRESH ARTICHOKES ARE A TREAT, but also a lot of work. Canned artichoke hearts, available in most grocery stores, allow you to enjoy the delicious taste of artichokes anytime without the fuss. I like to serve this dip with rice crackers or Pita Chips *(page 261)*.

1	garlic clove, peeled
1	shallot, peeled
2	tablespoons lemon juice
½	cup vegan mayonnaise
1	tablespoon apple cider vinegar
¾	cup great northern beans
¼	teaspoon sea salt
½	teaspoon powdered mustard
¼	teaspoon ground white pepper
1	4-ounce can chopped green chiles
2½	cups canned artichoke hearts, drained

With food processor running, drop in garlic clove and process until minced. Turn off processor, scrape down sides of bowl, add remaining ingredients except artichokes and process until well combined. Add artichokes and process briefly so that small chunks remain. Season to taste with additional salt and serve.

MAKES 3 cups

Creamy Miso Dressing

IN WINTER WE DRINK PIPING HOT MISO SOUP to cleanse the digestive system, replenish healthy intestinal flora, regulate cholesterol and flush away toxins. In spring we can gain the same health benefits from miso by using it in salad dressings or dips, as I've done here.

1   shallot, minced
1   garlic clove, minced
3   tablespoons lemon juice
2   tablespoons mellow white miso
2   tablespoons tahini
½   cup extra virgin olive oil
¼   cup water

Place all ingredients in food processor and pulse to combine. Store in airtight container in refrigerator for up to 5 days.

MAKES 1 cup

Lettuce Soup with Cilantro and Hot Sesame Oil

I ONCE HEARD A FAMOUS CHEF TALKING about making soup out of leftover salad greens. My initial reaction was not positive, but each spring as salad greens became abundant the idea started to intrigue me. It didn't take much experimentation to create this delicious soup that offers a surprising combination of light and refreshing taste with an added touch of heat.

6	dried shiitake mushrooms
6	cups water
1	leek, sliced into thin rounds
1	cup bamboo shoots
2	cups corn, fresh or frozen
¼	cup chopped fresh cilantro
2	cups thinly sliced romaine lettuce (or other variety)
5	dashes hot sesame oil
7	dashes ume plum vinegar

Place mushrooms in pot with water, bring to boil, reduce heat and simmer 20 minutes. Remove mushrooms, discard stems, thinly slice caps and return to pot. Add leek, bamboo shoots and corn. Simmer 3 minutes. Add cilantro and lettuce, stir and continue to cook until greens have wilted (about 3 minutes). Add hot sesame oil and vinegar and serve. Refrigerate leftovers in airtight container for up to 4 days.

SERVES 6

Cream of Asparagus Soup

ALL WINTER LONG I SUSTAIN MYSELF with hearty soups that I can practically eat with a fork. By early spring, I transition to more delicate soups like this one. This nondairy soup has the richness of a cream soup without the fat and guilt, and is surprisingly easy to make. If you're preparing this soup for guests, do so in advance, chill for 3–4 hours to allow flavors to blend, then reheat, garnish and serve.

2–3 bunches asparagus
  (about 6 cups chopped)

2 tablespoons extra
  virgin olive oil

2 garlic cloves, minced

3 leeks, white parts
  only, chopped

½ cup rolled oats

3 cups rice milk or soy milk

½ teaspoon dried dill

Sea salt and white pepper

1 teaspoon mellow
  white miso per serving

Chopped fresh parsley
  for garnish

Bend each piece of asparagus near the tough dried end until it snaps off at its natural breaking point. Discard ends, wash remaining asparagus, cut into 2-inch pieces and set aside.

In large pot over medium heat, sauté garlic and leeks in olive oil until soft (2–3 minutes). Add asparagus, oats, milk and dill, then add enough water to just cover asparagus. Bring to boil, reduce heat, cover and simmer until asparagus is soft (about 10 minutes). Remove from heat and cool slightly.

Purée soup using a handheld blender. Add water if thinner soup is desired. Season to taste with salt and white pepper. Dissolve miso in just enough water to make it liquid. Stir into each serving. Garnish with parsley and serve.

Note: Miso is added to individual servings rather than to the full pot so you can reheat leftover soup without destroying miso's living enzymes.

SERVES 6

Corn Chowder

MY DAUGHTER FELL IN LOVE WITH CORN CHOWDER at our local natural food store, but I didn't feel good about all the heavy cream and butter that was in it. I developed this completely nondairy recipe, and she loves it even more than the other. It can be put together in no time, and is a welcome treat year-round.

1   tablespoon extra virgin olive oil

1   onion, chopped

4   stalks celery, chopped

2   carrots, chopped

2   medium potatoes, peeled and chopped

¼   cup mirin

½   teaspoon sea salt

3½ cups corn, fresh or frozen

5   cups rice milk or soy milk, plus more if needed

Sea salt and freshly ground black pepper

In large pot over medium heat, sauté onion in olive oil until soft (about 3 minutes). Add celery, carrots, potatoes, mirin and salt and sauté 3–4 minutes. Add corn and enough milk to just cover ingredients. Bring to boil, reduce heat, cover and simmer 20 minutes. Remove from heat and purée gently with a handheld blender. Add water as needed to achieve desired consistency. Season to taste with salt and pepper and serve.

SERVES 4

Sweet Potato, Corn and Kale Chowder

WHEN I PREPARE DINNER, I try to make sure there's something for everyone. This chowder accomplishes that in one pot and is a colorful variation on an old favorite. It cooks up quickly and provides a balanced meal rich in nutrients all in one satisfying bowl.

1   tablespoon grapeseed oil

1   small onion, diced

3   stalks celery, diced

3   carrots, diced

3   medium sweet potatoes, peeled and diced

3   cups corn, fresh or frozen

2   teaspoons dried thyme

2   cups vegetable stock

2   cups rice milk, plus more if needed

2   tablespoons cashew butter, dissolved in ¼ cup hot water

1   bunch kale, chopped into small pieces

Sea salt and freshly ground black pepper

In large pot over medium heat, sauté onion in oil until soft (about 3 minutes). Add celery, carrots, sweet potatoes, corn, thyme and stock. Simmer 5 minutes. Add enough rice milk to cover the vegetables. Bring to boil, reduce heat and simmer until vegetables are soft (about 20 minutes). Remove from heat and add dissolved cashew butter. Partially purée using a handheld blender. Add kale, return to heat, thin to desired consistency with water or stock and cook until kale is tender. Season to taste with salt and pepper and serve.

SERVES 6

My Favorite Miso Soup

I CALL THIS WATER SOUP! Because miso is a living food and boiling destroys its beneficial enzymes, I prepare the ingredients in water and then add miso to the individual servings. That way I can save any leftover soup in the refrigerator, and reheat it without worrying about harming miso's living enzymes. This easy-to-make soup combines the medicinal benefits of sea vegetables, miso and tofu.

6   cups water

3   carrots, chopped

12   ounces extra firm silken tofu, diced

1   3-inch strip wakame, broken into small pieces

Dash of tamari or shoyu

¼   cup miso (I like traditional barley, chickpea or mellow white)

2–3 scallions, chopped

In large pot over high heat bring water to boil. Add carrots, tofu, wakame and tamari, reduce heat and simmer 10 minutes. Remove from heat.

In separate bowl, dissolve miso in ⅓ cup water. Ladle soup into individual bowls and stir 1 generous tablespoon of dissolved miso into each serving. Top with chopped scallions and serve.

SERVES 4

Fresh Herb Salad with Lemon and Olive Oil

LEMON IS A POWERFUL ALLY when it comes to maintaining balance, increasing alkalinity and cleansing. This simple salad features fresh greens, abundant herbs and lemon, which means it's quick and easy to prepare and big on flavor and texture – supporting the theory that less is often more!

---

2   heads romaine lettuce

2   cups mixed fresh herbs (such as parsley, cilantro, fennel, dill, basil or mint)

¼   cup chopped scallions

DRESSING

¼   cup extra virgin olive oil

¼   cup lemon juice

⅛   teaspoon sea salt

Plenty of freshly ground black pepper

Tear lettuce into pieces and place in large salad bowl with fresh herbs and scallions. In separate bowl, whisk together dressing ingredients. Pour over salad and toss to coat evenly. Serve immediately.

SERVES 4

Spring Greens with Apricot Vinaigrette

TO BE APPEALING AND DELICIOUS, a tossed salad does not need to be decorated with fancy fixings, nor do hearty greens need to be sautéed or steamed. These greens and herbs fall into both categories. Experiment with different combinations and don't be afraid to try something new. A trip to your local farm or farmers' market can fill your salad bowl with all sorts of unusual findings. You might also enjoy this salad with some sliced avocado and pumpkin seeds.

---

6 cups spring greens and herbs of choice (try baby chard, bok choy, fennel, fennel fronds, escarole, romaine lettuce, mustard greens, parcel,* dill, chives, garlic scapes or other)

VINAIGRETTE

1 garlic clove, minced

1 small shallot, minced

Juice of 2 Meyer lemons

¼ cup apricot juice

¼ cup balsamic vinegar

½ cup extra virgin olive oil

1 tablespoon maple mustard

2 tablespoons maple syrup

Pinch of sea salt

Tear greens into pieces and place in large bowl. In separate bowl, whisk together vinaigrette ingredients. Pour vinaigrette over greens, toss and serve.

*See "What's That?" (page 32), for information on this leafy herb.

SERVES 6

Fennel and Orange Salad

THE COMBINATION OF CRISP FRESH FENNEL with cool refreshing citrus is a treat. The coriander adds just a bit of savory flavor to give this dish even more depth and interest. Be sure to tear your mint leaves rather than cut them to keep the edges from turning brown.

---

4   navel oranges

½   small red onion, very thinly sliced

1   fennel bulb, halved, cored and thinly sliced

¼   cup fresh mint leaves, torn

DRESSING

1   teaspoon ground coriander

2   tablespoons fresh orange juice

2   tablespoons red wine vinegar

¼   teaspoon sea salt

3   tablespoons extra virgin olive oil

Remove zest from 2 oranges and set aside. Remove peels and white outer skins from all 4 oranges. Slice into rounds, or separate into segments.

Bring 2 cups water to boil. Place sliced onion in small bowl, cover with boiling water, let sit 30 seconds, then drain well.

In large bowl, toss together orange segments, fennel, red onion, mint leaves and orange zest. In separate bowl, whisk together all dressing ingredients and pour over salad. Toss to coat evenly and serve.

SERVES 6

Watercress, Daikon and Avocado Salad with Mustard Seed Dressing

WATERCRESS AND DAIKON MAKE THIS SALAD super cleansing and heart healthy, and their bitter flavors and crisp textures are balanced perfectly by the smooth richness of avocado and mustard. I like to use the stems and leaves of watercress and remove only the dried stem ends (or the wet root ball if it is hydroponically grown).

1	large bunch watercress, chopped
1	large daikon, peeled and julienned
1	avocado, peeled, pitted and diced
½	cup toasted pumpkin seeds

DRESSING

1	tablespoon yellow mustard seeds
1	tablespoon lemon juice
1	teaspoon light miso
1	tablespoon brown rice syrup
1	tablespoon prepared mustard
2	tablespoons extra virgin olive oil

In large bowl, combine watercress, daikon, avocado and pumpkin seeds.

In dry pan, over medium heat, toast mustard seeds until they start to pop. Remove from heat and let cool slightly.

In medium bowl, whisk together remaining dressing ingredients. Stir in mustard seeds, pour over vegetables and fold gently to coat evenly. Serve at room temperature.

Note: If you prefer salad chilled, refrigerate vegetables and dressing separately and toss together just before serving.

SERVES 4

Chopped Salad with Shallot Poppy Seed Dressing

THIS COLORFUL AND COOLING SALAD features a variety of tastes, including fresh asparagus, bitter greens, creamy avocado and salty olives to yield a delightful dish that is always a crowd pleaser. It pairs nicely with grilled chicken or fish.

8	stalks asparagus
1	avocado
1	tablespoon lemon juice
2	heads endive, chopped
2	bunches watercress, chopped
1	head radicchio, chopped
1	cup halved cherry tomatoes
1	orange bell pepper, chopped
½	cup kalamata olives, pitted
3	stalks celery, chopped
½	red onion, chopped

DRESSING

1	cup extra virgin olive oil
⅓	cup red wine vinegar
1	small shallot, minced
½	teaspoon sea salt
¼	cup agave nectar
2	tablespoons poppy seeds

GARNISH

1	cup toasted pumpkin seeds

Bend each piece of asparagus near the tough dried end until it snaps off at its natural breaking point. Discard ends, wash asparagus and cut into 1-inch pieces. Place in bowl. Bring 3 cups water to boil. Pour over asparagus, let sit 1 minute, the drain.

Cut avocado in half and remove pit. Scoop out flesh, cut into chunks and toss with lemon juice to prevent browning.

In large bowl, combine asparagus, avocado and all remaining salad ingredients. Set aside.

In separate bowl, combine all dressing ingredients except poppy seeds and whisk by hand or with handheld blender. Stir in poppy seeds.

Pour dressing over salad and toss to combine. Top with toasted pumpkin seeds and serve.

SERVES 8 as a side salad

Caesar Salad

I LOVE A TRADITIONAL CAESAR SALAD, so it was absolutely essential that I develop this heart-healthy version. If you are not opposed to fish, the addition of one anchovy or two tablespoons of dried bonito to the dressing makes this already delicious faux-Caesar taste even more like the real deal.

2	heads romaine lettuce
½	cup kalamata olives, pitted
1	cup sourdough croutons (or variety of choice)

DRESSING

8	ounces soft silken tofu
3	tablespoons apple cider vinegar
3	tablespoons lemon juice
1	tablespoon mellow white miso
3	garlic cloves, minced
1	teaspoon grated fresh ginger
2	teaspoons brown rice syrup
1	cup extra virgin olive oil
1	tablespoon chopped fresh parsley

Tear lettuce into bite-size pieces and place in large salad bowl. Top with olives and croutons.

In food processor, whip tofu until smooth. Add remaining ingredients and process until combined. Pour dressing over salad, toss and serve.

SERVES 6

Carrot Raisin Salad

THIS RECIPE TAKES A DELI COUNTER FAVORITE and spices it up with orange zest and grated fresh ginger. To prevent the nuts from getting soggy, add them just before serving this dish.

¼ cup nuts or seeds (try walnuts, sunflower seeds or pine nuts)

3 cups grated carrots

½ cup raisins

4 cups boiling water

Zest and juice of ½ lemon

Juice of 2 oranges

Zest of 1 orange

1 teaspoon grated fresh ginger

Pinch of sea salt

Preheat oven to 250°F.

Place nuts or seeds on parchment-lined baking sheet and roast until fragrant and lightly browned (watch closely to avoid burning). Remove from oven and set aside.

In large bowl, combine carrots and raisins. Cover with boiling water, let sit for 30 seconds, drain, rinse with cold water and drain completely. Stir in juices, zests, ginger and salt. Refrigerate until cold. Sprinkle with toasted nuts or seeds and serve.

SERVES 4

Crispy Sesame Carrots

THESE LIGHT AND CRISPY CARROTS WERE A BIG HIT with my family from the start and are a far cry from typical cooked carrots. If you have a food processor, the slicing disc will make your prep time minimal. It will feel like you are preparing an enormous amount of carrots, but they shrink dramatically in the oven. In fact, you may want to make extra to compensate for all the ones you and your family members will sneak before you get this dish to the table!

---

2 pounds carrots, sliced into thin rounds

1 tablespoon extra virgin olive oil

1 tablespoon toasted sesame oil

Coarse sea salt

2 tablespoons toasted sesame seeds

2 tablespoons toasted black sesame seeds

Preheat oven to 350°F.

In large sauté pan over medium heat, sauté sliced carrots in olive oil until just soft (about 6 minutes). Remove from heat, toss with toasted sesame oil and sea salt to taste, spread out on cookie sheet and bake 30 minutes. Check frequently and move carrots around to prevent burning. Remove from oven, toss with sesame seeds and serve.

SERVES 4

Seared Fennel
with Meyer Lemon

MEYER LEMONS ARE A SPRING DELICACY and infuse this dish with a sweet citrus tang. If Meyer lemons are not available, substitute regular lemons plus a dash of orange juice. Use a cast-iron skillet to sear this dish to perfection.

3	fennel bulbs
2	tablespoons extra virgin olive oil
1	shallot, thinly sliced

Zest and juice of
1 Meyer lemon

1	tablespoon chopped fennel fronds (if available)

Coarse sea salt

Cut fennel bulbs into wedges and steam until just soft. Remove from heat and set aside.

In large skillet over medium-high heat, sauté shallot in olive oil for 2 minutes. Add fennel (wedges) and sear 2 minutes. Add lemon zest and juice, chopped fennel fronds and a pinch of salt. Sauté 1 more minute. Remove from heat and serve.

SERVES 6

Sautéed Fennel and Asian Greens with Ginger and Apricot

WHILE I AM A NUT FOR KALE AND COLLARD GREENS most of the year round, I am every bit as nutty for the Asian greens that are so bountiful at the farm in early spring. Bok choy, pac choy, tatsoi, Napa cabbage, Chinese broccoli. . .the selection is overwhelming, and all of the varieties work in this recipe, so have fun experimenting.

---

2   tablespoons extra virgin olive or grapeseed oil

2   tablespoons grated fresh ginger

½   fennel bulb, halved, cored and thinly sliced

8   cups sliced Asian greens

3   tablespoons apricot all-fruit jam

1   tablespoon tamari

In large skillet or Dutch oven over medium heat, sauté ginger in oil 1 minute. Add fennel and sauté 5 minutes or until fennel is soft and translucent. Stir in apricot jam and tamari, add greens and gently fold until greens are bright green. Remove from heat and serve.

SERVES 4

Roasted Portobello Sandwich with Sun-dried Tomato Aioli

BITING INTO A PORTOBELLO MUSHROOM is about as far as you can get from the sprouts and shaved-carrot vegetarian sandwich of the past. Not only is this sandwich delicious, but it really gives you something to sink your teeth into! The aioli will last five days in the refrigerator, so make extra to accommodate dipping with crudités after your sandwiches are gone.

Portobello mushrooms
(1–2 per serving)

Extra virgin olive oil

1   tablespoon minced fresh
Italian herbs of choice
(oregano, basil, thyme
or parsley)

Sea salt and freshly ground
black pepper

Sourdough bread
(2 slices per serving)

Roasted red peppers, sliced
into ½-inch strips

Avocado, thinly sliced

Romaine lettuce

Spicy honey mustard

AIOLI

6   sun-dried tomatoes

1   garlic clove, peeled

1½ cups grapeseed oil
mayonnaise

2   tablespoons fresh Italian
herbs of choice

Pinch of sea salt

PREPARING AIOLI

Soak dried tomatoes in hot water 15 minutes or until soft. With the food processor running, drop in garlic. Process until minced. Squeeze excess water from tomatoes and add them along with mayonnaise to processor. Scrape down sides of the bowl as needed and process until smooth. Add herbs and salt and process lightly. Transfer to container and refrigerate to allow flavors to blend.

ROASTING PORTOBELLOS

Preheat oven to 400°F.

Line cookie sheet with parchment paper. Wipe mushrooms with a damp towel to clean. Discard stems and rub smooth side with olive oil. Place smooth side on cookie sheet and sprinkle insides with Italian herbs, pepper and a pinch of salt. Roast for 8–10 minutes until soft. Remove and set aside.

ASSEMBLING

Slice bread and lightly toast. Spread aioli on toast and top with roasted portobello, roasted red pepper, avocado and lettuce. Spread mustard on second piece of toasted bread, top sandwich and serve warm.

Mango Sesame Tatsoi

LOOK FOR THIS TENDER SPRING SPECIALTY Chinese cabbage at your local organic farm or Asian grocery store. If you can't find it, you can substitute baby bok choy or pac choy instead.

---

6   heads tatsoi (whole)
1   tablespoon grapeseed oil
2   tablespoons water
1   tablespoon toasted
    sesame seeds

DRESSING

½   mango, peeled, pitted
    and finely chopped
1   shallot, minced
2   tablespoons brown
    rice vinegar
2   tablespoons toasted
    sesame oil
¼   cup grapeseed oil
Sea salt

In medium bowl, whisk together all dressing ingredients and set aside.

Rinse greens, keeping heads together (do *not* trim off ends or separate leaves). Heat oil in large skillet over medium-high heat. Add tatsoi and sauté 1 minute. Add water and steam tatsoi until just soft and bright green (2–3 minutes). Remove from heat, arrange greens on serving dish and top with mango dressing. Sprinkle with sesame seeds and serve.

SERVES 6

Seared Artichokes
with Red Pepper Aioli

ARTICHOKES ARE REASONABLY PRICED AND PLENTIFUL in the spring. For years I would stuff each leaf with herbed bread crumbs. Many hours (and pounds) later, I switched to this light and easy approach. Marinating the artichokes infuses them with flavor and the aioli makes for an impressive finish.

4   whole artichokes

¼   cup extra virgin olive oil

1   tablespoon lemon juice

2   tablespoons chopped fresh herbs of choice (tarragon, dill, lemon balm, marjoram or rosemary)

Sea salt and freshly ground black pepper

RED PEPPER AIOLI

1   garlic clove, peeled

2   tablespoons extra virgin olive oil

1½   cups grapeseed oil mayonnaise

3   roasted red peppers, skins and seeds removed

Sea salt and freshly ground black pepper

PREPARING ARTICHOKES

Bring large pot of water to boil.

Remove tough lower leaves from artichokes, and trim and peel the stems. Snip off sharp ends of leaves, and cut off top ½-inch where leaves are tight. Place artichokes in pot, reduce heat, cover and cook until cores are just soft (about 20 minutes). Drain cooking water, rinse with cold water and set upside-down to drain completely.

Once artichokes have cooled, gently squeeze out any remaining water and carefully cut in half from stem to tip. Scoop out and discard fuzzy choke.

In medium bowl, whisk together olive oil, lemon juice, herbs and salt and pepper to taste. Place prepared artichokes in sealable container, pour in marinade, seal, shake gently and refrigerate at least 1 hour, shaking container occasionally to redistribute marinade.

PREPARING AIOLI

With the food processor running, drop in garlic clove and process until minced, scraping down sides as needed. Add remaining ingredients and purée until smooth. Transfer to separate container, cover and refrigerate until ready to use.

FINISHING

Preheat griddle, grill or cast-iron skillet to high and sear artichokes until grill lines show (1–2 minutes per side). Serve hot with aioli on the side.

SERVES 8

Asparagus with Mustard Vinaigrette and Toasted Pecans

VINAIGRETTES ARE A SIMPLE WAY to season fresh steamed vegetables, and toasted pecans finish this dish with an extra-special touch. Toasting the nuts and preparing the vinaigrette in advance will allow you to put this dish together in no time.

---

2 pounds asparagus
¾ cup pecans

VINAIGRETTE

½ cup extra virgin olive oil
¼ cup red wine vinegar
1 tablespoon prepared mustard
⅛ teaspoon sea salt
Freshly ground black pepper

Preheat oven to 300°F.

In small bowl, whisk together vinaigrette ingredients and set aside.

Place pecans on parchment-lined cookie sheet and toast until fragrant and lightly browned. Remove from oven and set aside to cool.

To prepare asparagus, bend each piece near the tough dried end until it snaps off. Discard ends and steam asparagus until it turns bright green (about 3 minutes). Remove from heat and place on a serving dish. Drizzle with vinaigrette, top with toasted pecans and serve.

SERVES 4

Bok Choy and Chickpeas with Cashews

THIS IS ONE OF MY FAVORITE BREAKFAST DISHES! No, that is not a typo. I love the uplifting energy of greens first thing in the morning, and the addition of chickpeas and cashews makes this dish one that satisfies me and keeps me energized for hours.

1	tablespoon extra virgin olive oil
1	tablespoon grated fresh ginger
1	tablespoon Bragg Liquid Aminos
1	tablespoon mirin
1	cup cooked chickpeas
6	heads baby bok choy, chopped into large pieces
½	cup toasted cashews

In large skillet over medium heat, sauté ginger in olive oil 1 minute. Add liquid aminos, mirin and chickpeas and sauté 2 minutes. Add bok choy and sauté another 2–3 minutes or until greens are just tender. Remove from heat, top with toasted cashews and serve.

SERVES 4

Artichokes, Fennel and Olives over Penne

THE STRONG FLAVORS OF THIS DISH demand pasta for balance and to hold it all together. This is one of those recipes that simply cannot fail. Don't worry if you don't have all of the ingredients – any bitter greens (try dandelion greens, mustard greens or watercress) will substitute beautifully for the arugula. For an even bigger change, serve over polenta instead of penne.

1	pound penne pasta
3	tablespoons extra virgin olive oil
1	onion, diced
2	garlic cloves, minced
1	cup canned artichoke hearts, quartered
½	cup kalamata olives, pitted
1	fennel bulb, halved, cored and thinly sliced
1	bunch arugula
1	cup chopped tomatoes, fresh or canned
¼	cup chopped fresh parsley
1	tablespoon lemon juice
Sea salt and freshly ground black pepper	

Cook penne according to directions on package. Rinse, drain and return to pot. Drizzle with 1 tablespoon olive oil and set aside.

Meanwhile, in large pot over medium heat, sauté onion and garlic in 2 tablespoons olive oil until soft (about 3 minutes). Add artichokes, olives, fennel and arugula. Sauté until heated through (about 5 minutes). Add tomatoes and sauté another 2 minutes. Add parsley and lemon juice. Season to taste with salt and pepper. Remove from heat and serve over pasta.

SERVES 4

Swiss Chard with Roasted Golden Beets and Sweet Peas

THIS RECIPE WILL WORK with any of your favorite dark leafy greens. In spring and early summer we devour peas right out of their shells. They are as sweet as candy and a wonderful addition to any salad or vegetable dish. During the cooler months, try frozen sweet peas or edamame beans. To make this dish a complete meal, serve it over couscous or French lentils.

3–4	golden beets
2	tablespoons extra virgin olive oil
1	Vidalia onion (or other sweet variety), diced
3	bunches Swiss chard
1	cup fresh peas removed from their shells
Coarse sea salt and freshly ground black pepper	

Preheat oven to 425°F.

Wrap beets loosely in foil, place in baking dish and bake 45 minutes or until soft throughout. Remove from oven and set aside. When cool enough to touch, open foil and gently peel away skins by pressing them firmly with your thumb. Trim away blemishes and cut beets into bite-size pieces.

In large skillet over medium heat, sauté onion in 1 tablespoon olive oil until soft (about 3 minutes). Add chard and toss gently until it starts to wilt (1–2 minutes). Add beets and peas and sauté another minute until peas are heated through and bright green. Remove from heat and toss with remaining tablespoon olive oil. Season to taste with salt and pepper and serve.

SERVES 6

Sesame Brussels Sprout Sauté

I GREW UP DESPISING BRUSSELS SPROUTS but started cooking them on rare occasions after marrying a man who grew up loving them. I did not expect to fall for them myself, but once I learned the secret – to slice them thinly – I too became a believer! Using this recipe, I've since converted more non-lovers than I can count. A cast-iron skillet makes the difference in browning them to perfection.

16	Brussels sprouts
4	garlic cloves, minced
2	tablespoons extra virgin olive oil
1	tablespoon mirin
1	tablespoon toasted sesame oil
¼	cup toasted sesame seeds

Sea salt

Prepare Brussels sprouts by trimming off dry ends and peeling away any damaged outer leaves. With stems down, thinly slice and set aside (be sure to keep any leaves that fall off).

In large skillet over medium heat, sauté garlic in olive oil until soft. Add Brussels sprouts and mirin and sauté for 15 minutes. Don't skimp on the time as extended cooking helps them caramelize and take on incredible flavor. If they start to burn or stick to the bottom of the skillet, add water 1–2 tablespoons at a time to deglaze pan. Continue sautéing until sprouts start to brown. Remove from heat, toss with toasted sesame oil and sesame seeds. Season to taste with salt and serve.

SERVES 4

Sautéed Yams with Ginger and Lime

SOME RECIPES, LIKE BAKED SWEET POTATO FRIES, are so delicious and easy to make that we prepare them all the time. But after years of eating them no other way, I needed a change. I was looking for a new take on sweet potatoes, while also trying to save myself the time it took to bake the fries. It worked! The combination of flavors and texture of this dish exceeded my expectations and spiced up my week's menu.

2   tablespoons extra virgin olive oil

2   tablespoons grated fresh ginger

1   red onion, minced

2   large yams or sweet potatoes, peeled and shredded

3   tablespoons lime juice

1   teaspoon ground nutmeg

Sea salt and freshly ground black pepper

In large sauté pan over medium heat, sauté ginger and onion in olive oil until soft (about 5 minutes). Add shredded yams and lime juice, and increase heat to medium-high. Stir continuously and sauté 5–7 minutes or until yams start to soften. Season with nutmeg, and salt and pepper to taste. Cook 2–3 minutes longer. Remove from heat and serve.

SERVES 6

Sweet and Sour Stir-Fry

THE SECRET TO MAKING NOODLES that stand up to stir-frying is to cook your noodles and then chill them before using. This is one of the first stir-fry combinations I ever made, and it has endured the test of time. It's colorful, simple and full of flavor.

½	pound udon or soba noodles
1–2	heads broccoli
3	carrots, diced
1	tablespoon grapeseed oil
3	garlic cloves, minced
1	tablespoon grated fresh ginger
1	cup snow peas, ends trimmed and strings removed
1	cup pineapple chunks
2	tablespoons brown rice vinegar
2	tablespoons mirin
2	tablespoons Bragg Liquid Aminos
2	tablespoons toasted sesame oil
¼	cup toasted sesame seeds

Cook noodles according to directions on package. Drain in colander and rinse thoroughly under cold water. Place colander on a plate and refrigerate.

PREPARING VEGETABLES

Bring 2–3 cups water to boil. Cut broccoli florets into bite-size pieces. Peel and discard tough outer stems and cut remaining stems into chunks. Place prepared carrots and broccoli in bowl, cover with boiling water and let sit 2 minutes. Drain, rinse with cold water and set aside.

STIR-FRYING

Heat wok or skillet over medium-high heat. Add grapeseed oil, garlic and ginger and cook 1 minute. If anything starts to stick, add 1 tablespoon water. Add broccoli, carrots and snow peas, stir and cook 2–3 minutes. Add pineapple, 1 tablespoon vinegar, 1 tablespoon mirin, 1 tablespoon liquid aminos and cook 1 minute longer. Remove vegetables from wok and set aside.

Pour remaining tablespoon of vinegar, mirin and liquid aminos into empty wok. Fold in chilled noodles until evenly coated and heated through. Drizzle with 1 tablespoon sesame oil. Transfer noodles to serving dish. Toss vegetables briefly in hot wok to reheat, drizzle with remaining tablespoon toasted sesame oil and spoon vegetables over noodles. Top with sesame seeds and serve.

SERVES 6

Stir-Fried Broccoli with Arame

IF YOU'RE NEW TO SEA VEGETABLES, arame is a great place to begin. Not only does it have a mild flavor and aroma, but it only needs to be soaked before using. This simple recipe is bursting with flavor, as well as alkalinizing calcium and minerals. Be sure to sauté the mushrooms for the full time to bring out their rich flavor.

½   cup dried arame

1   small bunch broccoli, cut into bite-size pieces

1   tablespoon extra virgin olive oil

½   red onion, diced

1   tablespoon tamari

10   shiitake mushroom caps, thinly sliced

Soak arame in 2 cups of water for 20 minutes. Drain and set aside. Steam broccoli until bright green and tender. Set aside.

In large skillet over medium heat, sauté onion in oil until soft and translucent (about 5 minutes). Add tamari and stir to deglaze the pan and caramelize the onions. Add mushrooms and sauté for 10 minutes. Deglaze pan with 1 tablespoon water at a time as needed. Add broccoli and arame, cook to heat through and serve.

SERVES 4

Arame and Sunflower Seeds

I TEND TO EAT MORE ARAME than other sea vegetables because it is so easy to prepare and goes so nicely with everything from carrots and salad greens to brown rice and aduki beans. Sunflower seeds are a rich source of protein, vitamins D, B-complex and E and make a nutritionally packed crunchy addition to this recipe. If you don't plan to finish eating this dish in one sitting, add seeds only to individual servings so that the sunflower seeds don't get soggy as leftovers.

1	cup dried arame
1	teaspoon grapeseed oil
2	tablespoons mirin
1	tablespoon brown rice syrup
½	teaspoon ume plum vinegar
1½	cups roasted salted or tamari-roasted sunflower seeds

Soak arame in 4 cups of water for 20 minutes and drain.

In large skillet over medium heat, sauté arame in oil for 3 minutes.

In small bowl, whisk together mirin, brown rice syrup and vinegar. Pour over arame and stir to blend, then sauté another minute. Remove from heat, add sunflower seeds and serve.

SERVES 6

Seaweed and Cabbage Sauté

I CRAVE THIS POWERHOUSE COMBINATION in the spring for its incredible cleansing and healing properties. Sea vegetables are loaded with easily absorbable calcium. Cabbage is a tonic for the stomach and digestive system, a blood alkalinizer, and a rich source of antioxidants, vitamins and minerals. Now that's strong medicine! This recipe doubles easily and keeps 4–5 days.

1	cup dried arame
1	teaspoon grapeseed oil
1	red onion, cut into wedges
3	carrots, cut into matchsticks
½	small cabbage (green or Napa), thinly sliced
2	tablespoons tamari
2–3	dashes ume plum vinegar
1	tablespoon toasted sesame oil

Soak arame in 4 cups of water for 15 minutes, drain well and set aside.

In large skillet over medium heat, sauté onion in grapeseed oil until translucent (3 minutes). Add carrots and sauté another 2–3 minutes. Add cabbage and tamari and sauté until all vegetables have softened. Add seaweed and cook to heat through. Remove from heat, add vinegar and toasted sesame oil and serve warm or chilled.

SERVES 6

Gingered Arame with Snow Peas

FEW FOODS PROVIDE THE NUTRITIONAL PUNCH and cleansing ability of sea vegetables. Chock-full of calcium and minerals, alkalinizing to the blood, and highly regarded for its ability to break down tumors and support thyroid function, arame is a powerful ally to health and well-being.

1	cup dried arame
½	red onion, cut into wedges
1½	cups snow peas, cut into matchsticks
8	radishes, cut into matchsticks

DRESSING

1	tablespoon grated fresh ginger
2	teaspoons brown rice vinegar
2	teaspoons brown rice syrup
1	teaspoon tamari
2	tablespoons toasted sesame oil

Soak arame in 4 cups of water for 20 minutes. Drain and place in pot with enough fresh water to cover plus 2 tablespoons tamari. Bring to boil, reduce heat and simmer uncovered 15 minutes. Drain well and set aside.

In medium bowl, combine onion, snow peas and radishes. Bring 4 cups water to boil, pour over vegetables, let sit 1 minute then drain. Rinse vegetables under cold running water and drain completely. Combine with arame and set aside.

PREPARING DRESSING

In small sauté pan, combine ginger, vinegar, syrup and tamari. Cook over medium heat 1–2 minutes until blended and heated through. Remove from heat and stir in sesame oil. Pour over arame mixture, toss to combine and serve.

SERVES 6

Multibean Salad with Fresh Herbs

THIS RECIPE IS A PERFECT WAY TO EXPERIMENT with a variety of fresh herbs – whether from your garden, the farm or the grocery store. Look for one of the many different varieties of basil, or perhaps fennel, dill, chervil, lemon balm or lovage. This one salad can provide a whole education on herbs and herb combinations. It did for me!

1   cup green beans, trimmed
1   cup cooked black beans
1   cup cooked chickpeas
1   cup cooked kidney beans

VINAIGRETTE

½   small red onion, finely chopped
¼   cup extra virgin olive oil
1   tablespoon red wine vinegar
1   teaspoon lemon juice
1   teaspoon chopped fresh rosemary
1   tablespoon chopped fresh basil
1   teaspoon chopped fresh chives
1   tablespoon chopped fresh parsley
1   tablespoon prepared mustard
Freshly ground black pepper

Cut green beans in half and place in bowl. Add black beans, chickpeas and kidney beans. Bring 4 cups water to boil, pour over beans and let sit 1 minute. Drain, rinse under cold running water and drain completely.

In separate bowl, whisk together all vinaigrette ingredients. Pour over beans, toss to coat and serve.

SERVES 6

Marinated Aduki Beans

ADUKI BEANS ARE ONE OF THE EASIEST LEGUMES to digest, but their tangy flavor makes them a challenge to pair with other foods. Some of my favorite matches for aduki beans include millet, sweet brown rice, winter squash, root vegetables and collard greens. I'm always looking for new ways to get aduki beans into my diet so I can take full advantage of their ability to detoxify the body and support the kidneys. Serve this recipe with Ginger Sesame Greens *(page 267)* and pan-roasted millet *(page 14)*, or enjoy it chilled for lunch or a snack.

---

2 cups cooked aduki beans

2 carrots, cut into matchsticks

½ red onion, thinly sliced

2 tablespoons toasted sesame seeds

MARINADE

2 teaspoons toasted sesame oil

1 tablespoon grated fresh ginger

1 teaspoon tamari

1 teaspoon brown rice vinegar

1 teaspoon brown rice syrup

Rinse cooked beans in colander and drain well. Place carrots and onion in bowl. Bring 2 cups water to boil, pour over carrots and onion, let sit 1 minute, then drain. Add carrots and onions to beans. Toss to combine.

In separate bowl, whisk together all marinade ingredients. Pour over bean mixture and stir to coat evenly. Let sit 10–15 minutes to allow flavors to combine. Stir again before serving.

SERVES 4

Tempeh Salad

I LOVED TUNA AS A CHILD AND I STILL DO, but as an adult I worry about the high levels of mercury and other toxins found in large fish like tuna and swordfish. I enjoy this tuna-inspired salad every bit as much as that from the can, if not more. Your body will appreciate the significant health benefits from the addition of kelp – known for its rich supply of minerals and its ability to dissolve masses in the body, balance hormones and support thyroid function.

1   8-ounce package tempeh
1   carrot, shredded
½   red onion, minced
2   tablespoons sweet
      pickle relish
½   fennel bulb, chopped
1   tablespoon capers
1   tablespoon chopped
      fresh parsley
2   tablespoons grapeseed
      oil mayonnaise
1   tablespoon powdered kelp
Sea salt and freshly ground
      black pepper

Cut tempeh into 3–4 large pieces and steam 10 minutes. Remove from heat and cool slightly. Crumble or chop tempeh into small pieces. Add remaining ingredients and stir to combine. Season to taste with salt and pepper. Serve at room temperature or chilled.

VARIATIONS

Serve on a bed of romaine lettuce, in a wrap or even in a grilled soy or rice cheese sandwich.

SERVES 4

Crispy Chickpea Fritters

THESE RICH AND TASTY FRITTERS ARE SURPRISINGLY VERSATILE.
Each combination highlights them in a completely different way. Enjoy them alongside Sautéed Garlic Greens *(page 266)*, Chopped Salad with Shallot Poppy Seed Dressing *(page 54)* or Caesar Salad *(page 55)*. Or serve them as an appetizer with a bowl of spaghetti sauce for dipping. Whichever pairing you choose, you won't be disappointed.

---

2 cups chickpea flour

3 cups water

1 tablespoon coarse sea salt

¼ red onion, minced

1 carrot, grated

2 tablespoons minced fresh rosemary

2 tablespoons extra virgin olive oil

Grapeseed or extra virgin olive oil for frying

In large pot over no heat, combine chickpea flour, water, salt, onion, carrot, rosemary and olive oil. Whisking continuously, turn heat to medium and continue to whisk until mixture becomes quite thick (about 15 minutes). Remove from heat and either whisk by hand or with a handheld blender to smooth out any lumps.

Oil 9 x 12-inch glass casserole and spread mixture evenly across the bottom. Cool slightly, cover and refrigerate until firm (about 2 hours). Remove from refrigerator, cut into thin strips and gently remove strips from casserole.

Preheat oven to 250°F.

Heat large sauté pan (cast-iron gives a nice crispy outer crust), cover the bottom in oil and fry fritters 2–3 minutes per side. Remove from heat and place on paper towels to absorb excess oil. Keep fritters warm in the oven while you fry up the remaining strips. Serve immediately.

SERVES 6–8

Mochi Dumplings

THIS RECIPE GREW OUT OF my children's addiction to dumplings from one of our favorite Chinese restaurants. It simply wasn't realistic to order in dumplings every night, so I came up with this quick and easy version. This traditional dumpling filling is a perfect complement to baked mochi. Plus, we all love watching the mochi puff in the oven and stuffing our own squares.

---

1   12.5-ounce block mochi, cut into 2-inch squares

1   tablespoon extra virgin olive oil

½   onion, diced

1   tablespoon grated fresh ginger

1   carrot, grated

1   cup cabbage, thinly sliced

¼   cup thinly sliced shiitake mushroom caps

1   tablespoon tamari or shoyu

1   tablespoon mirin

DIPPING SAUCE

2   tablespoons tamari

1   tablespoon toasted sesame oil

1   teaspoon brown rice vinegar

Sesame seeds and scallions for garnish

Preheat oven to 400°F.

In small bowl, combine all dipping sauce ingredients and set aside.

In large skillet over medium heat, sauté onion and ginger in olive oil for 2–3 minutes. Add carrot, cabbage, mushrooms, tamari and mirin and sauté 5–7 minutes or until vegetables are soft. Remove from heat and set aside.

Place mochi squares 2 inches apart on parchment-lined cookie sheet. Bake 10–12 minutes (until squares puff and lightly brown). Remove from oven, cool slightly, slice open mochi puffs and fill with stuffing. Press to close and seal the dumplings. Serve warm with dipping sauce.

MAKES 10–12 dumplings

Inca Red Quinoa
with Currants

THIS DEEP RED VARIETY OF QUINOA has every bit as much protein as traditional ivory quinoa, plus a nuttier taste, more texture and less bitterness. I eat quinoa year-round and prefer it to other grains because it is so light. You may also like the red variety mixed with the traditional ivory, paired with Spring's bitter greens or stuffed into Fall's sweet winter squashes.

1   cup Inca red quinoa

1½ cups water

Pinch of sea salt

2   tablespoons extra virgin olive oil

1   small yellow onion, chopped

½   cup currants

2   tablespoons dried summer savory

Ume plum vinegar

Rinse quinoa well and drain. Place quinoa in pot or rice cooker with water and salt and bring to boil. Cover, reduce to simmer and cook until water is absorbed (about 15 minutes). Remove from heat, cool slightly, then fluff with fork.

In large skillet, heat 1 tablespoon olive oil over medium heat, add onion and sauté until soft (about 3 minutes). Add currants and savory and sauté another 3 minutes or until currants soften. Add cooked quinoa and fold to combine all ingredients. Add remaining tablespoon of olive oil and 3–4 dashes of vinegar and serve.

SERVES 6

Millet Black Bean Patties with Corn

THIS IS ANOTHER FAMILY FAVORITE AND WEEKLY STAPLE. I keep organic frozen corn in my freezer year-round just for recipes like this one. Try these patties with salsa, ketchup or the accompaniment of your choice. We like them with sweet potato fries and a salad. Leftovers are great stuffed into a pita with lettuce and tomato.

1 cup millet
2½ cups water
Grapeseed oil for frying
1 medium onion, minced
¼ teaspoon sea salt
¼ teaspoon chile powder
1 tablespoon paprika
2 teaspoons ground cumin
1½ cups cooked black beans
1 cup corn, fresh or frozen
Freshly ground black pepper or hot pepper sauce
½ cup cornmeal

PREPARING MILLET

Rinse millet, place in sauté pan over medium heat and toast for 3–4 minutes, stirring continuously. When millet begins to take on a nutty aroma, add water, cover, reduce heat to low and cook until all water is absorbed (about 25 minutes). Remove from heat and set aside to cool slightly.

PREPARING PATTIES

In large skillet or Dutch oven over medium heat, sauté onion in grapeseed oil until soft (about 3 minutes). Add salt, chile powder, paprika and cumin and stir to combine. Add black beans and corn and remove from heat. Add cooked millet and mash together. Season to taste with pepper, then stir in cornmeal a little at a time until batter is stiff.

Preheat large skillet over medium heat (I use cast-iron to yield a nice crispy crust) and add 2 tablespoons of oil. Scoop and form mixture into 2-inch balls. Working in batches and adding more oil as needed, place balls in skillet and press down to form patties. Repeat until skillet is full. Fry 3–4 minutes per side. Place cooked patties on a baking sheet, cover with foil and keep warm in the oven until ready to serve.

Note: To reheat leftovers, wrap in foil and bake at 350°F for 15 minutes.

MAKES 10 hearty patties

Barley with Lemon and Herbs

BARLEY IS PARTICULARLY STRENGTHENING and easy to digest. It also helps to lower cholesterol and tone the liver and stomach. Whole barley is minimally processed and nutritionally far superior to pearl barley. Barley is particularly acidic, so be sure to allow time for presoaking.

---

1   cup whole barley
2¼ cups vegetable stock
1   thumb-size piece kombu

DRESSING
¼   cup extra virgin olive oil
¼   cup lemon juice
1   garlic clove, minced
1   tablespoon chopped
    fresh parsley
½   teaspoon minced
    fresh rosemary
1   tablespoon fresh
    lemon thyme leaves
2   teaspoons dried
    summer savory
Sea salt and freshly ground
    black pepper

Soak barley at least 1 hour, then drain and cook with stock and kombu *(see complete directions on page 14).*

While barley is cooking, in medium bowl whisk together dressing ingredients and set aside for flavors to blend.

Remove cooked barley from heat and discard kombu. Fluff with fork, toss with dressing and serve.

SERVES 6

Wild Rice Pilaf

WILD RICE IS ACTUALLY A GRASS, not a grain, and is extremely high in protein. I like this recipe in the fall and winter, too, but in spring it provides a nice transition away from winter's heavier, more warming grain dishes. This sweet and savory recipe complements a variety of flavors and dishes and is perfect for holiday entertaining.

---

1   cup wild rice

½   cup brown basmati rice

Pinch of sea salt

3   cups vegetable stock or water

2   tablespoons extra virgin olive oil

6   shallots, diced

2   tablespoons mirin

3   stalks celery, diced

½   pound cremini mushrooms, diced

1   tablespoon minced fresh rosemary

½   cup dried cranberries

½   cup toasted slivered almonds

¼   cup chopped fresh parsley

Sea salt and freshly ground black pepper

Place wild and basmati rice together in pot or rice cooker with stock or water and pinch of salt. Bring to boil, cover, reduce heat and simmer until liquid is absorbed (about 40 minutes). Remove from heat and set aside.

In large skillet over medium heat, sauté shallots in olive oil and mirin until translucent. Add celery, mushrooms and rosemary and sauté 2–3 minutes. Mix in cranberries. Fluff rice with fork and fold into vegetable mixture. Cook another 2 minutes to heat through. Remove from heat, fold in almonds and parsley, season to taste with salt and pepper and serve.

SERVES 6

Mediterranean Pasta with Greens

I'VE BEEN MAKING THIS DISH FOR YEARS. It wasn't as much a recipe as it was a quick and easy meal that everyone liked. It could be because the ingredients were always available in my kitchen, or simply because it was so yummy and satisfying.

1	pound penne or fusilli
3	tablespoons extra virgin olive oil
3	garlic cloves, minced
1	small onion, chopped
1	tablespoon dried basil
2	teaspoons dried oregano
1½	cups cooked chickpeas
2	cups canned diced tomatoes with their liquid
2	tablespoons tomato paste
¼	cup mirin
1	small bunch kale, chopped into bite-size pieces

Sea salt and freshly ground black pepper

Chopped fresh parsley for garnish

Cook pasta according to directions on package. Rinse, drain and return to pot. Drizzle with 1 tablespoon olive oil and set aside.

In large Dutch oven over medium heat, sauté garlic and onion in 2 tablespoons olive oil until soft (about 3 minutes). Add basil, oregano, chickpeas, tomatoes, tomato paste and mirin. Sauté 5 minutes longer. Add kale, then cover and cook 3 minutes or until soft. Uncover and stir to combine all ingredients. Season with salt and lots of pepper and toss with pasta. Cook to heat through, garnish with parsley and serve.

SERVES 6

Blueberry Kanten with Cashew Cream

A KANTEN IS A VEGETARIAN JELLED DESSERT made with fruit and agar. It's hard to believe that these delicate little flakes can have such tremendous healing and alkalinizing power, but agar is loaded with minerals and is particularly detoxifying. Agar is also cooling and calming to the gastrointestinal tract. Hardly sounds like dessert anymore!

KANTEN

3   cups apple or pear juice
3   tablespoons agar flakes
Pinch of sea salt
1   tablespoon lemon juice
    or apple cider vinegar
2   cups frozen blueberries

CASHEW CREAM

2   cups apple juice
2   cups lightly toasted cashews
3   tablespoons maple syrup

TOPPING

Cookie crumbs of choice

PREPARING KANTEN

In large pot over medium-high heat, bring juice to boil. Reduce heat to low and stir in agar flakes, salt and lemon juice or cider vinegar. Continue stirring until flakes have dissolved. Remove from heat, add blueberries and transfer to 9 x 13-inch glass casserole. Refrigerate until firm (about 45 minutes). Remove from refrigerator and purée with handheld blender until texture is similar to mousse.

PREPARING CASHEW CREAM

In small pot over medium-high heat, bring apple juice to boil. Remove from heat and cool slightly. Place cashews and syrup in food processor and process 10–15 seconds. With the processor running, slowly add juice a little at a time until you have the desired texture (you may not need all the juice).

ASSEMBLING

Fill bottom of 6–8 parfait glasses with a layer of kanten, add a layer of cashew cream, top with cookie crumbs and serve.

SERVES 6–8

Crispy Rice Squares

MOMS HAVE BEEN MAKING crispy rice treats forever. I feel good about this healthy version, and have never met a child (or adult) who doesn't love these. If you are allergic to nuts, use sunflower butter instead of cashew butter.

½ cup brown rice syrup

½ cup maple syrup

½ cup cashew butter

¼ cup semi-sweet dark chocolate chips

3 cups crispy brown rice cereal

½ cup toasted sesame seeds

In medium Dutch oven over medium-low heat, combine syrups and cashew butter until smooth. Add chocolate chips and stir until melted. Fold in rice cereal and sesame seeds and stir to coat everything. Press stiff batter into 8 x 8-inch casserole and refrigerate until firm (at least 20 minutes). Cut into squares and serve or store in airtight container.

MAKES 1–1½ dozen 1-inch squares

Raisin Nut Bars

THESE YUMMY BARS CAME INTO BEING when we realized that our daughter was sensitive to wheat, corn, soy and dairy – all of my usual baking staples. They're delicious even if you have no food allergies!

1½ cups raisins
1 cup brown rice flour
1 cup rolled oats
1 cup toasted walnuts, chopped
½ teaspoon sea salt
¼ cup canola oil
¼ cup maple syrup
Apple juice as needed

Preheat oven to 350°F.

Place raisins in bowl and cover with boiling water. Let sit 10 minutes or until soft. Drain and press out excess water. Chop softened raisins and set aside.

In large bowl, combine flour, oats, walnuts and salt. In separate bowl, whisk together oil and syrup. Pour wet ingredients over dry ingredients, add raisins and mix until blended. You want the dough to be moist enough to just stick together. Add apple juice if needed to achieve this consistency.

Oil 6 x 9-inch glass casserole and press in batter so it sticks together and is consistently thick throughout. Pre-cut into squares and bake 25 minutes. Remove from heat and let cool completely before removing from pan. Store in airtight container.

MAKES 16 squares

Mixed Berry Couscous Cake

THIS CAKE IS NOT THE LIGHT AND FLUFFY KIND, but you're going to love it anyway. When chilled, couscous remains quite moist, dense and cool, making for a cake that's refreshing and guilt-free. Enjoy it as a dessert, snack or even for breakfast.

7   cups apple juice

2   tablespoons vanilla extract

1   cup maple syrup

3   cups couscous

3   tablespoons agar powder or flakes

3–4 cups berries of choice

Fresh mint leaves for garnish

In medium pot over no heat, whisk together 6 cups apple juice, vanilla and ½ cup maple syrup. Bring to boil, add couscous and stir until thick. Remove from heat, rinse 9-inch springform pan with cool water (to prevent sticking) and pour in cooked couscous. Smooth top and set aside.

In small pot over medium heat, dissolve agar in remaining cup of apple juice. Add remaining ½ cup maple syrup and stir continuously until agar dissolves. Fold in berries and remove mixture from heat. Place couscous cake on large plate or cookie sheet (to catch fruit drippings), and immediately pour berry mixture over couscous. Refrigerate at least 1 hour to chill and to allow fruit topping to set. Before serving, remove cake from pan by cutting around the edge of the cake to break the seal with the pan. Garnish with fresh mint leaves and serve.

Chocolate Coconut Granola Bites

THESE TREATS ARE SIMPLE TO PREPARE but far from innocent. Cut them into bite-size pieces, as they are quite rich.

2½ cups Maple Nut Granola *(page 260)*, or other type of granola

½ cup dried cranberries

1½ cups semi-sweet dark chocolate chips

2 cups shredded unsweetened dried coconut

Spread granola and cranberries evenly over bottom of ungreased 8 x 8-inch glass casserole. In small pot over low heat, melt chocolate bits until smooth. Drizzle evenly over granola and smooth top so all granola is covered. Sprinkle with coconut and refrigerate to cool and set. Using a sharp knife, cut into small pieces and serve.

Banana Coconut Chocolate Chip Cookies

FINALLY A RECIPE FOR THOSE OVERRIPE BANANAS other than banana bread! Gluten is the protein in wheat that is quite sticky and helps hold baked goods together. In this wheat-free recipe, bananas bind the ingredients and also add significant sweetness so that only a small amount of maple syrup is needed.

2	bananas, mashed
¼	cup canola oil
¼	cup maple syrup
½	teaspoon vanilla extract
1	cup rolled oats
⅔	cup brown rice flour
¼	teaspoon baking soda
½	cup shredded unsweetened dried coconut
Pinch of sea salt	
¼	cup semi-sweet dark chocolate chips

Preheat oven to 350°F.

In medium bowl, combine bananas, oil, syrup and vanilla. In separate medium bowl, combine oats, flour, baking soda, coconut and salt. Add the banana mixture to the dry ingredients and blend until just combined (do not overstir). Fold in chocolate chips.

Line cookie sheet with parchment paper and drop batter by the heaping teaspoon onto sheet. There is no need to roll, flatten or shape the mounds. Place in oven and bake 14 minutes or until lightly browned. Remove from oven and place directly on wire rack to cool.

MAKES 1½ dozen cookies

Love is to the heart what the summer
is to the farmer's year – it brings to harvest
all the loveliest flowers of the soul.

AUTHOR UNKNOWN

Summer

The selection and taste of freshly picked organic produce is never more exciting than in summer and it appeals to my every sense. Everywhere I look are infinite varieties of heirloom tomatoes, beets in every color, potatoes as small as pebbles and seemingly bottomless baskets filled with green beans. The berries are sweeter than sugar, and herbs and flowers fill the air with their aromatic bouquet. Food artisans of all kinds display their specialty breads, oils, cheeses, vinegars and relishes, giving me a glimpse into their kitchens and a taste of new flavors and ideas to spice up my own menu. Eating seasonally helps me maintain balance with the environment, and purchasing local organic produce allows me an even greater sense of harmony and supports a sustainable approach to farming and nutrition. A conversation with the farmer directs me to unusual varieties, freshly harvested picks and the "cream of the crop." There is no better way to get to know your food – from seed to table.

SUMMER

Herbal Iced Tea

YEARS AGO, MY NATUROPATH PRESCRIBED a concoction of herbs for me to brew that I quickly coined "dirt tea." Over the years, this much more pleasant brew evolved. Not only does it replenish my adrenals, but it is refreshing and satisfying too. Feel free to experiment with other herbs to make your own unique brew.

---

10   cups water
¼   cup dried nettles
1   tablespoon dried
      red clover flowers
2   tablespoons dried
      rosemary
3   tablespoons chamomile
2   tablespoons dried
      peppermint leaves
1   tablespoon agave nectar

In large pot, bring water to boil. Remove from heat, stir in herbs and agave, and set aside to brew and cool for at least 1 hour. Pour tea through fine mesh strainer into pitcher. Discard herbs, chill tea and enjoy.

MAKES 10 cups

Fruity Balsamic Vinaigrette

THERE ARE SO MANY DIFFERENT JUICES AND NECTARS available in stores these days. You can achieve completely different vinaigrettes by substituting mango, cranberry or even carrot juice for the apricot juice in this recipe.

---

1   garlic clove, peeled

1   small shallot

Juice of 2 Meyer lemons
     or 1 large regular lemon

¼   cup apricot juice

¼   cup balsamic vinegar

½   cup extra virgin olive oil

1   tablespoon maple mustard
     or honey mustard

2   tablespoons maple syrup

Pinch of sea salt

Combine all dressing ingredients in food processor or with handheld blender. Vinaigrette will keep refrigerated for up to 1 week.

MAKES 1½ cups

Herbed Aioli

THIS DIP IS A SPRING AND SUMMER MUST. Serve it with crudités or steamed artichokes, or wrap it up in a sheet of nori with avocado, smoked salmon, carrot and cucumber. Create a whole new dip simply by substituting different seasonal herbs. The possibilities are endless.

---

1   garlic clove, peeled
1½ cups grapeseed oil
    mayonnaise
¼   cup fresh chives
¼   cup fresh basil

With food processor running, drop in garlic and mince. Turn off processor, scrape down sides, add remaining ingredients and pulse until herbs are chopped. The goal is a white dip with green flecks — not a green dip. Serve immediately or refrigerate for up to 5 days.

MAKES 1½ cups

Traditional Guacamole

I'M NOT SURE WHAT MAKES RECIPES "TRADITIONAL." Perhaps it means that they've been passed from generation to generation, or maybe there is simply no dispute about the ingredients. What I do know is that there is a little Mexican restaurant in Chicago where they make the most outstanding guacamole right at your table, and ever since tasting their fresh guacamole I've been making this one.

3	large avocados, peeled, pitted and chopped (save the pits)
2	garlic cloves, minced
¼	cup chopped red onion
2	tomatoes, diced
2	jalapeños, seeded and minced
¼	cup chopped fresh cilantro
3	tablespoons lime juice

Sea salt to taste

Place all ingredients in medium bowl, gently mash to the desired texture and serve.

If you do not plan to serve guacamole immediately, place pits on top of mixture to keep it from turning brown. Cover and refrigerate. Before serving, remove pits and stir briefly.

MAKES 2 cups

Jícama Strawberry Guacamole

IF YOU'VE NEVER TASTED A WATERMELON RADISH, you've been missing out. Its sweet taste and vibrant pink flesh will have you hooked in no time. If watermelon radishes aren't available, don't deprive yourself of this guacamole. Tomatillos, cipollini onions or even peaches make great substitutes.

1 cup diced strawberries

½ cup peeled and diced jícama

1 watermelon radish, peeled and diced

2 avocados, peeled, pitted and diced (save the pits)

1 jalapeño, seeded and minced

Juice of 2 limes

¼ teaspoon sea salt

¼ teaspoon garlic powder

2 tablespoons extra virgin olive oil

In large bowl, combine strawberries, jícama, watermelon radish, avocados and jalapeño. In separate bowl, combine lime juice, salt, garlic powder and olive oil. Pour over strawberry mixture and stir until combined. If not serving immediately, place avocado pits in bowl to keep dip from turning brown. Cover and refrigerate. Before serving, remove pits and stir briefly.

MAKES 3 cups

Mango Salsa

THIS SALSA ADDS ZEST TO A VARIETY OF DISHES and is a great accompaniment to baby bok choy, asparagus and grilled fish. I also serve it solo with chips for a refreshing change from its more ordinary cousins tomato salsa and guacamole. If you don't care for mango, try preparing this salsa with peaches, nectarines or papaya.

---

1   mango, pitted, peeled and diced

1   avocado, peeled, pitted and diced (save pit)

1   tomato, diced

¼   cup peeled and diced jícama

1   jalapeño, seeded and minced

1   small red onion, minced

¼   cup chopped fresh cilantro

Juice of 1 lime

1–2 tablespoons extra virgin olive oil

Sea salt

In large bowl, combine mango, avocado, tomato, jícama, jalapeño, onion and cilantro. Fold in lime juice. Add olive oil (1 tablespoon at a time) until desired consistency is reached. Season with sea salt to taste, place pit on top of mixture to keep avocado from turning brown, cover and set aside (or chill) to allow flavors to blend. Remove pit before serving.

MAKES 3 cups

Black Bean, Corn and Tomato Salsa

SERVE THIS SUMMER SALSA with corn chips, tacos, rice and beans or grilled chicken or fish. The delicate texture and sweet taste of fresh native tomatoes are compromised by refrigeration, so I serve this salsa at room temperature.

¾ cup cooked corn, fresh or frozen

2 garlic cloves, minced

¾ cup cooked black beans

1½ cups chopped fresh tomatoes

¼ cup chopped green bell pepper

¼ cup chopped fresh cilantro

2 jalapeños, seeded and minced

2 tablespoons lemon juice

1 tablespoon extra virgin olive oil

Sea salt and freshly ground black pepper

Hot pepper sauce

If using frozen corn, place in strainer and run under hot water to thaw.

In large bowl, combine garlic, beans, corn, tomatoes, peppers, cilantro and jalapeños. Add lemon juice and olive oil. Season to taste with salt, pepper and hot pepper sauce. Set aside for 1 hour to allow flavors to blend.

MAKES 3 cups

Tofu Sour Cream

IF YOU HAVE ELIMINATED DAIRY from your diet, there are certain basic recipes, like this one, that you want to make sure you have when you need them. This simple nondairy sour cream whips up in a snap and is a great addition to tacos, burritos, refried beans and so much more. For a more traditional sour cream, eliminate the jalapeño.

8	ounces firm or extra-firm silken tofu
2	tablespoons lemon juice
3	tablespoons canola oil
2	teaspoons brown rice vinegar
½	teaspoon sea salt
½	jalapeño, stem and seeds removed

In food processor, whip tofu until smooth. Add remaining ingredients and process until pepper is minced and ingredients are well combined. Chill before serving.

MAKES 1 cup

Gazpacho

I ONCE READ THAT THE EASIEST WAY to make gazpacho was to put the previous night's leftover salad in a blender with tomato juice, lemon juice, salt and pepper. I've yet to try it, so if you're feeling daring, please let me know how it comes out! Meanwhile, I'll stick to this tried-and-true recipe that gets rave reviews every time.

4–6 tomatoes

1   small red onion, minced

1   green bell pepper, minced

1   cucumber, diced

1   garlic clove, minced

2   tablespoons chopped
    fresh parsley

2   tablespoons chopped
    fresh basil

2   tablespoons chopped
    fresh cilantro

4   cups tomato juice

2   tablespoons lemon juice

2   tablespoons balsamic
    vinegar

Dash of hot pepper sauce

¼   cup extra virgin olive oil

Sea salt and freshly ground
    black pepper

Fresh parsley and lemon
    for garnish

Bring large pot of water to boil. Drop in tomatoes, let sit 30 seconds, drain and set aside. When cool, peel away skins by applying pressure and pushing them off with your thumbs. Dice and return to empty pot.

Add remaining ingredients and adjust seasoning to taste with hot pepper sauce, salt and pepper. Stir until evenly combined. Cover and refrigerate. Serve cold with a wedge of lemon and a sprig of parsley.

SERVES 6

Carrot Fruit Soup

SIMPLE, REFRESHING AND BEAUTIFUL! This sweet soup is a perfect way to start any summer barbecue.

---

1   cantaloupe

2   peaches, peeled and
     cut into chunks

1   mango, peeled and
     cut into chunks

1½   cups carrot juice

1   tablespoon fresh
     lemon juice

¼   teaspoon ground cloves

Pinch of sea salt

Blueberries for garnish

Halve cantaloupe, scoop out seeds, remove outer skin and cut melon into chunks. Place in large pot and add peaches, mango, carrot juice, lemon juice, cloves and sea salt. Bring to simmer and cook 3 minutes to soften fruit. Purée with handheld blender and refrigerate for 1 hour or longer. Garnish with blueberries and serve.

SERVES 6

Traditional Coleslaw

OKAY, SO MAYBE THIS COLESLAW isn't 100 percent traditional, but it's a cinch to make and one of my favorite ways to enjoy greens in the summer. Everyone who tries it ends up asking for the recipe. Ume plum vinegar wilts the vegetables perfectly and makes them easier to digest as well. Feel free to add your favorite vegetables for color and variety.

1   large green cabbage
Ume plum vinegar
1   fennel bulb, thinly sliced
3   carrots, julienned
½   red onion, finely chopped
1   watermelon radish, julienned (or 6 small radishes cut into matchsticks)
¼   cup grapeseed oil mayonnaise

Cut cabbage in half, core and slice into thin strips. Place in large bowl and sprinkle generously with ume plum vinegar to coat. Cover and let sit for at least 2 hours. Stir cabbage every 30 minutes to redistribute vinegar. Cabbage will break down considerably.

When done, transfer cabbage to a large colander, rinse and drain well to remove excess vinegar. Dry and return to bowl. Add fennel, carrots, onion and radish and toss to combine. Fold in mayonnaise to evenly coat, then serve. Store leftovers for up to 5 days refrigerated in airtight container.

Note: Drain excess water from leftovers before serving each day, as cabbage will continue to break down.

SERVES 6

Asian Coleslaw

CHINESE CABBAGE MAKES THIS SLAW SOMETHING SPECIAL, and
I just love the added zip of fresh ginger in this cool and refreshing salad.
Because these cabbages are more delicate than regular green cabbage,
there's no need to wilt them first. Just slice up your vegetables, add your
dressing and chill.

---

3   cups thinly sliced bok choy
    or pac choy

4   cups thinly sliced
    Napa cabbage

1   carrot, julienned

2   cups julienned snow peas

1   cup julienned red
    bell pepper

2   tablespoons toasted
    black sesame seeds

2   tablespoons toasted
    white sesame seeds

DRESSING

1   tablespoon extra
    virgin olive oil

1   tablespoon toasted
    sesame oil

2   teaspoons ume
    plum vinegar

1   tablespoon tamari

2   teaspoons grated
    fresh ginger

In large bowl, combine cabbages, carrot, peas and peppers. In separate
bowl, whisk together all dressing ingredients. Pour over cabbage
mixture and toss to coat evenly. Refrigerate 10–20 minutes to help
flavors blend. Before serving, toss again and top with toasted
sesame seeds.

SERVES 8

Heirloom Tomato Salad

THE KEY TO ENJOYING DELICIOUS NATIVE TOMATOES is never to refrigerate them as doing so makes their flesh mealy. There are so many varieties of heirloom tomatoes that I feel bad leaving some out. Reds, yellows, oranges, stripes, ringed plums…it's a veritable symphony of tomatoes.

5	cups heirloom tomatoes of choice
2	small cucumbers
1	avocado, peeled and pitted
¼	red onion, finely chopped
¼	cup chopped fresh basil
1	tablespoon red wine vinegar
2	tablespoons extra virgin olive oil

Sea salt and freshly ground black pepper

Chop tomatoes, cucumbers and avocado into bite-size pieces and combine in serving dish. In separate bowl, combine onion, basil, vinegar, oil, and salt and pepper to taste. Pour over tomatoes and serve.

Note: Combine green and purple varieties of basil for an especially beautiful presentation.

SERVES 6

Tangy Tomato and Tomatillo Salad

TOMATILLOS AND LIME JUICE GIVE this tomato salad a surprising and refreshing twist, and minced jalapeño gives it some extra zip. For a spicy yet refreshing summer meal, serve this with burritos, corn on the cob, fresh guacamole and chips.

4   cups small heirloom tomatoes (yellow peach variety are my favorites)

4   tomatillos, husked and quartered

½   watermelon radish, peeled and julienned

¼   cup chopped fresh cilantro

2   tablespoons lime juice

2   tablespoons extra virgin olive oil

1   jalapeño, seeded and minced

Coarse sea salt

Cut tomatoes into half-moons and place in serving dish with prepared tomatillos, radish and cilantro. In separate bowl, whisk together jalapeño, lime juice and olive oil. Pour over salad, sprinkle with coarse sea salt and serve.

SERVES 6

Baby Greens with Grilled Balsamic Pears

THIS SALAD REQUIRES SOME ADVANCE PLANNING to marinate and grill the pears, but it's worth the effort, especially once that first bite of balsamic pear melts in your mouth. Add tender baby greens and rich toasted walnuts and you'll be wishing you had made extra.

---

3   pears, cored and thinly sliced

¼   cup balsamic vinegar

2   tablespoons agave nectar

Pinch of sea salt

Extra virgin olive oil for grilling

6   cups baby salad greens

1   cup chopped toasted walnuts

1   avocado, peeled, pitted and thinly sliced

VINAIGRETTE

¼   cup walnut oil

2   tablespoons balsamic vinegar

2   shallots, minced

1   tablespoon maple syrup

1   teaspoon Dijon mustard

Sea salt and freshly ground black pepper

PREPARING PEARS

Place pears in shallow dish. In separate bowl, whisk together vinegar, agave nectar and a pinch of sea salt. Pour mixture over pears and marinate 15 minutes.

Heat grill or grill pan to medium, brush cooking surface with olive oil and place pears on grill. Grill each side 3 minutes or until soft. Remove from heat and set aside.

PREPARING VINAIGRETTE

In small bowl, whisk together all vinaigrette ingredients.

ASSEMBLING SALAD

Place greens in large bowl, drizzle with vinaigrette and toss to coat. Compose individual servings of greens on each plate and top with nuts, avocado slices and grilled pears. Serve immediately.

VARIATION

Grilled pineapple completely changes this recipe, but is equally tasty. Prepare pineapple by cutting away the outer skin, slicing into rounds and grilling 3 minutes per side. Place on plate, top with baby greens and avocado slices (no walnuts), drizzle with vinaigrette and serve.

SERVES 6

Baby Spinach Salad with Mustard Vinaigrette

THIS SALAD BURSTS WITH FLAVOR AND COLOR and makes a perfect complement to grilled fish or chicken. For a quick and easy lunch, try tossing with half a cup of great northern or navy beans.

---

6 cups loosely packed baby spinach

1 cup de-stemmed and sliced strawberries

¼ cup toasted pumpkin seeds

VINAIGRETTE

2 tablespoons red wine vinegar

¼ cup extra virgin olive oil

1 teaspoon agave nectar

1 teaspoon Dijon mustard

Pinch of sea salt

Place spinach and ½ cup strawberries in salad bowl. In small bowl, whisk together all vinaigrette ingredients. Pour over salad and toss to coat. Top with remaining strawberries and pumpkin seeds and serve.

SERVES 4

Grilled Cipollini Onions

THESE ONIONS ARE ONE OF THE MANY GREAT DISCOVERIES
passed on to me by my organic farmers. They are juicy, succulent and
irresistible just off the grill. Serve them tossed with other grilled vegetables
like zucchini and eggplant, with baby field greens in a salad, with steamed
beans or potatoes, sliced over grilled chicken or fish, or as a simple yet
elegant side dish as presented here.

As many cipollini onions
   as you like

Extra virgin olive oil

Lemon zest and juice

Coarse sea salt

Preheat grill to medium-high.

Place whole unpeeled onions directly on grill and cook until charred
on the outside and soft throughout. Remove from heat and set aside
until cool enough to handle, then gently squeeze the root end of each
onion so that the burnt outer peel slips off and the inside of the onion
pops out. Discard the outer skins and place the onions in a bowl.
Season to taste with olive oil, lemon juice, lemon zest and coarse sea
salt. Serve warm.

Fingerling Potatoes and Green Beans with Lemon Dill Dressing

THESE POTATOES HIT THE FARM STANDS IN AUGUST in the Northeast and come in shades of red, purple and yellow. I like to comb through the bin and find the smallest ones – some even as small as marbles! Combined with haricots verts or regular green beans, they make a beautiful addition to any summer meal. For a colorful vegetarian feast that's sure to please, serve this dish with corn on the cob and Heirloom Tomato Salad *(page 106)*.

---

2   pounds fingerling potatoes

2   pounds haricots verts or green beans, trimmed

DRESSING

1   garlic clove, minced

¼   cup extra virgin olive oil

1   tablespoon fresh lemon juice

3   tablespoons chopped fresh dill

1   tablespoon chopped fresh parsley

Sea salt and freshly ground black pepper

In large pot, steam potatoes until nearly cooked through. Add green beans and steam 2–3 minutes longer, until bright green and al dente. Remove from heat and drain water. In separate bowl, whisk together dressing ingredients. Drizzle over the potatoes and beans, fold gently to combine and serve warm or at room temperature.

SERVES 8

Green Beans and Sweet Corn with Summer Vinaigrette

THIS SIDE DISH WHIPS UP IN AN INSTANT and adds beautiful color, sweetness and a bit of crunch to any meal. I lengthen the season for this recipe with fresh-frozen organic sweet corn. To maintain the full flavor and texture of your tomatoes, refrain from refrigerating them.

1½ cups corn, fresh or frozen

2 pounds haricots verts or green beans, trimmed

1 cup orange pear-shaped or cherry tomatoes, halved

VINAIGRETTE

2 tablespoons extra virgin olive oil

2 tablespoons red wine vinegar

1 garlic clove, minced

2 tablespoons chopped fresh basil or lemon thyme

Splash of fresh lemon juice

Sea salt and freshly ground black pepper

If using fresh corn, steam until tender (about 5 minutes). Remove from steamer and set aside until cool enough to handle. Cut off kernels and set aside. If using frozen corn, add to pot with green beans for last minute of steaming.

In large pot, steam or boil green beans for 3 minutes or until bright green and just tender. Drain water, add corn and set aside. In small bowl, whisk together all vinaigrette ingredients and pour over beans and corn. Add tomatoes, toss and serve.

SERVES 6

Summer Rolls with Lemon Basil Pesto

MY DAUGHTER CAME HOME FROM SCHOOL one day with a bag full of lemon balm and the expectation that I would turn it into something spectacular – and so this recipe was born. Wrappers made with tapioca flour will soften more quickly and yield a more delicate tasting finished product. If you don't have wrappers, enjoy this refreshing pesto on grilled vegetables.

8–10 rice or tapioca
    spring roll wrappers

2   cups sprouts of choice,
    rinsed and patted dry

2   avocados, peeled, pitted
    and sliced lengthwise

1   large red beet, peeled
    and julienned

3   carrots, julienned

Shallow bowl or plate
    of hot water and towels

LEMON BASIL PESTO

1   cup fresh lemon balm

1   cup fresh basil leaves

½   cup fresh mint leaves

1   cup toasted pine nuts

½   cup extra virgin olive oil

½   teaspoon sea salt

Prepare all vegetables and lay everything out ready for assembly in the following order: wrappers, bowl of water, sprouts, avocados, beets, carrots.

PREPARING PESTO

In food processor, blend all pesto ingredients until fairly smooth. Place in bowl and add to the line-up between the sprouts and avocado.

ASSEMBLING

Place a towel in front of you. Put one wrapper in bowl with hot water until soft (about 45 seconds). Remove and place on towel – pat dry. Place sprouts centered along the edge closest to you. Spread pesto over sprouts. Top with avocado, beet and carrot. Wrap by folding up the edge closest to you, folding in the sides, then rolling toward the far edge. Leave rolls whole or slice in half and place on serving dish. Continue with remaining wrappers and filling and serve chilled or at room temperature.

MAKES 8–10

Pad Thai Summer Rolls with Tamarind Dipping Sauce

A TASTY TWIST ON A TRADITIONAL ASIAN ROLL. I like to play with different sauces and stuffings in my rolls and hope you'll feel inspired to do the same. For variety, try making these rolls with Peanut Sauce *(page 117),* a favorite among the women in my book club.

8	ounces rice noodles
8	Bibb lettuce leaves
4	scallions, thinly sliced
1	cup snow peas, thinly sliced
2	cups mung bean sprouts
1	cup chopped fresh cilantro, leaves and stems
½	cup chopped roasted peanuts
8	rice or tapioca spring roll wrappers

Shallow bowl or plate of hot water and towels

TAMARIND SAUCE

2	tablespoons tamarind concentrate
4	garlic cloves, minced
1	teaspoon red chili paste
2	tablespoons sucanat
2	tablespoons lime juice
2	tablespoons peanut butter
3	tablespoons toasted sesame oil

Cook rice noodles according to directions on package, drain and set aside. Lay out ingredients for assembly into rolls in the following order: wrappers, bowl of water, lettuce, noodles, scallions, snow peas, bean sprouts, cilantro, peanuts.

PREPARING SAUCE

In medium bowl, dissolve tamarind in ¼ cup of hot water and remove any seeds. Add garlic, chili paste, sucanat, lime juice, peanut butter and sesame oil. Purée with handheld blender until thick and smooth. Add to line-up of ingredients after the noodles.

ASSEMBLING

Lay out towel in front of you. Put one wrapper in bowl of hot water until soft (about 45 seconds). Remove and place on towel and pat dry. Place lettuce leaf centered along the edge closest to you. Add ingredients on top of lettuce as they are arranged – noodles, sauce, scallion, snow peas, bean sprouts, cilantro and peanuts. Wrap by folding up the edge closest to you, then folding in the sides and rolling tightly toward the far edge. Place on serving dish and continue with remaining wrappers and filling. Serve with extra sauce for dipping.

MAKES 8

Golden Beet and Snap Pea Salad

I LOVE FRESH BEETS IN THE SUMMER, but dread working with red beets that stain my hands and kitchen. These golden beets leave you stain-free and are even sweeter than their red cousins. Believe me, nobody else likes cooking with beets either, so you'll get big points for preparing this dish for family and friends!

4–5 golden beets
2   cups snap peas
2   cups frisée

DRESSING

¼   cup extra virgin olive oil
3   tablespoons chopped
      fresh dill
1   tablespoon maple syrup
Juice of 1 lemon
Coarse sea salt and freshly
      ground black pepper

Place whole beets in large pot of boiling water and cook until tender throughout when pierced with knife (about 20 minutes). Drain water and set aside until cool enough to handle. Holding beets under cold water, gently push away outer skins. Cut away root ends and any blemishes, slice into wedges and set aside.

To prepare snap peas, pinch stems and pull down to remove ends and strings. Place in mixing bowl and blanch with boiling water for 30 seconds. Drain and rinse with cold water. Return to mixing bowl, combine with beets and set aside.

In small bowl, whisk together all dressing ingredients, pour over beets and peas and toss to combine.

Arrange beets and peas on bed of frisée and serve.

SERVES 6

Grilled Vegetables with Pasta

THIS RECIPE IS A FEAST FROM THE FARM. Select whatever looks best to you, grill it on a skewer or in a grilling basket and toss it with pasta and herbs. You simply can't go wrong.

---

1 orange bell pepper

1 zucchini

3 small Japanese eggplants

12 cherry tomatoes

12 cremini mushrooms

8 cipollini onions

1 pound pasta (fusilli or penne)

1 garlic clove, minced

3 tablespoons extra virgin olive oil

¼ cup chopped fresh basil

Sea salt and freshly ground black pepper

Preheat grill to medium-high. If you have a grilling basket, place on grill to heat. If using wooden skewers, pre-soak them in water for 15–20 minutes.

Cut pepper, zucchini and eggplants into 1-inch pieces. Wipe mushrooms clean with damp towel and remove stems. Peel onions and trim away root ends. Place all vegetables (including tomatoes) in large bowl, drizzle with 1 tablespoon olive oil and sea salt to taste. If using skewers to grill, place vegetables on them now.

Lower heat to medium and grill vegetables 5–7 minutes or until tender and slightly charred on the outside. Remove vegetables from grill, cover to keep warm and set aside.

Cook pasta according to directions on package. Drain cooked pasta, return to pot and add garlic, remaining 2 tablespoons olive oil, basil, salt and pepper. Add vegetables, season to taste with salt and pepper, toss to coat and serve.

SERVES 8

Rice Noodles and Peanut Sauce Rolled in Nori

NORI IS A STAPLE IN MY HOME. My kids love it plain (as does the dog), and we've tried just about everything we can think of as a filling. The spice of this peanut sauce is a nice complement to the cool, refreshing taste of the rice noodles. This healthy appetizer disappears quickly every time I make it. In fact, I usually make extra sauce and noodles and store them in the refrigerator for an easy snack the next day.

Nori sheets – one per person

Rice noodles or bean thread noodles – 1 cup cooked per serving

Pickled ginger

PEANUT SAUCE

¼ cup peanut butter

2 tablespoons coconut milk

1 teaspoon red chili paste

2 tablespoons maple syrup

2 tablespoons lime juice

1 teaspoon tamari

3 tablespoons toasted sesame oil or 2 tablespoons hot sesame oil

Water

Prepare noodles according to directions on package. Rinse with cool water, drain and set aside.

PREPARING SAUCE

Whisk together sauce ingredients. Thin with water to desired consistency.

ASSEMBLING

Place sheet of nori, shiny side down, on work surface or bamboo sushi rolling mat with the short edge facing you. Arrange a serving of noodles over the closest third of the sheet. Top with peanut sauce and pickled ginger. Carefully fold over end of nori where noodles are and continue rolling away from you to form a log. Seal by dampening edge with water. Let sit briefly until the nori is soft enough to cut easily. Cut into ½-inch pieces, arrange on platter and serve with peanut sauce.

SINGLE SERVING: 1 sheet nori yields 5–6 bite-size pieces

Arame Sauté

ARAME'S MILD FLAVOR makes it easy to add to a variety of recipes. This dish can be served fresh off the stove, at room temperature or chilled. Try it with a piece of grilled fish, with vegetable nori rolls or with marinated and grilled tofu or tempeh.

1	cup dried arame
1	teaspoon grapeseed oil
2	small cipollini onions, thinly sliced
4	carrots, julienned
1	cup peeled and julienned jícama
1	cup snow peas, trimmed
2	tablespoons mirin
1	tablespoon brown rice syrup
1	teaspoon tamari or shoyu
½	teaspoon ume plum vinegar
2	tablespoons water
¼	cup toasted sesame seeds

Place arame in bowl with enough water to cover. Soak 10 minutes. Rinse, drain and set aside.

In large skillet or Dutch oven over medium heat, sauté onions in grapeseed oil until soft (about 5 minutes). Add carrots, jícama, snow peas and mirin and cook 3 minutes longer until vegetables are al dente.

In small bowl, whisk together brown rice syrup, tamari, vinegar and water. Pour over vegetables and bring to simmer. Fold in arame and sauté 4 minutes to combine flavors and heat through. Remove from heat, top with sesame seeds and serve.

SERVES 4

Cucumber, Mango and Chickpea Salad

MY KIDS MADE UP THIS COMBINATION ONE NIGHT when my own creativity was running dry. I insisted that they needed to eat something green, and they opted for the cucumber with mango. I threw in the chickpeas for protein, and together we rummaged through the refrigerator (and garden) to find ingredients for our dressing. The rest is history.

2	medium cucumbers, peeled and diced
1	mango, peeled, pitted and diced
2	cups cooked chickpeas
¼	cup currants
¼	cup dried apricots, minced
½	cup fresh mint, chopped (orange mint or lemon balm are also nice)

DRESSING

2	tablespoons extra virgin olive oil
3	tablespoons lemon juice
1	small shallot, minced
	Sea salt and freshly ground black pepper

In large bowl, combine cucumbers, mango, chickpeas, currants, apricots and mint. In separate bowl, whisk together all dressing ingredients. Pour over salad, toss and serve.

SERVES 6

Chickpea and Cherry Tomato Salad with Cilantro Dressing

SUN GOLD CHERRY TOMATOES are super-sweet and provide a wonderful contrast in flavor and texture to chickpeas. Look for these and other heirloom varieties to make this simple salad extra-special. To maintain the delicious flavor and texture of your tomatoes, be sure *not* to refrigerate them.

---

2   pounds cherry tomatoes (mix varieties when possible)

3   cups cooked chickpeas

4–5 scallions, chopped

DRESSING

1   garlic clove, peeled

1   large bunch cilantro (about 1 cup)

½   cup extra virgin olive oil

2   tablespoons lemon juice

Sea salt and freshly ground black pepper

Cut tomatoes in half and place in large bowl with chickpeas and scallions.

With food processor running, drop in whole garlic clove and mince. Turn off processor, scrape down sides, add cilantro, olive oil, lemon juice, salt and pepper. Pulse to combine. Drizzle dressing over salad, toss to coat and serve.

SERVES 6

White Bean Salad with Roasted Tomatoes and Arugula

EVERY TIME I MAKE THIS RECIPE I am reminded of the August morning I spent at the farmers market in Waitsfield, Vermont, with my friend Pam. Together we selected local organic produce until our arms could carry no more. We returned home and got to work. The kitchen hummed as delicious aromas filled the house. It was a meal and a day to remember.

---

5 garlic cloves, peeled

2 sweet onions, cut into wedges (look for Walla Walla or Vidalia)

1 fennel bulb, halved, cored and chopped

5 carrots, chopped

Extra virgin olive oil

½ teaspoon coarse sea salt

Freshly ground black pepper

8 tomatoes, halved or quartered depending on size

3 cups cooked great northern or navy beans

6 cups arugula leaves

Preheat oven to 400°F.

In glass baking dish, combine garlic, onions, fennel and carrots. Drizzle with just enough olive oil to coat vegetables evenly. Toss with sea salt and plenty of pepper. Roast uncovered 20 minutes or until just tender. Remove from oven, fold in tomatoes and beans and return to oven to roast an additional 10 minutes or until tomatoes are soft.

Remove from oven, cover individual plates or large platter with fresh arugula, top with bean and vegetable mixture and serve.

SERVES 4

Black Bean Salad

THIS SALAD IS A SUMMER STAPLE IN MY HOME. It adds a splash of color to any meal, travels well for outings, hits the spot on the beach and tastes great alone or rolled into a burrito with avocados and salsa. Even if you don't have all the ingredients, go ahead and toss together what you have. With flavors like these, it's hard to go wrong!

4 cups cooked black beans

4 tomatillos, husked and diced

1 red bell pepper, diced

½ red onion, diced

1½ cups corn, fresh or frozen

2 jalapeños, seeded and minced

⅓ cup chopped fresh cilantro

1 teaspoon ground cumin

Juice of 1 lime

2 tablespoons extra virgin olive oil

Sea salt and freshly ground black pepper

Combine all ingredients in large bowl. Season to taste with salt and pepper. Set aside or refrigerate to allow flavors to blend, then serve cold or at room temperature. Store refrigerated in airtight container for up to 5 days.

SERVES 8

Black Bean Patties with Pineapple Guacamole

THESE DELICIOUS PATTIES can be made in advance and reheated in the oven before serving. For a complete meal, serve with a salad of mixed greens.

GUACAMOLE

1   cup diced fresh pineapple

1   cup peeled and diced jícama

1   roasted red pepper, minced

1   jalapeño, seeded and diced

2   avocados, peeled, pitted and diced (save pits)

½   red onion, minced

½   cup chopped fresh cilantro

2   tablespoons lime juice

1   tablespoon extra virgin olive oil

⅛   teaspoon sea salt

PATTIES

1   tablespoon ground golden flax seeds

2   garlic cloves, peeled

1   jalapeño, halved and seeded

¼   onion, peeled

½   cup chopped fresh cilantro

1½ teaspoons ground cumin

4   cups cooked black beans

⅔   cup breadcrumbs or cornmeal

Sea salt and freshly ground black pepper

Extra virgin olive oil or grapeseed oil for frying

PREPARING GUACAMOLE

Combine all ingredients in large bowl. Place pits on top of guacamole to keep avocados from browning. Cover and refrigerate to allow flavors to develop.

PREPARING PATTIES

Soak ground flax in bowl with 3 tablespoons water for 20 minutes.

With the food processor running, drop in garlic cloves, then jalapeño and then onion. Turn off processor, scrape down sides and process again until minced. Add cilantro and cumin and pulse briefly. Add 2 cups black beans and bread crumbs or cornmeal and process until just combined. Overprocessing will make your mixture too mushy. Transfer mixture to large bowl. Fold in soaked flax and remaining 2 cups of black beans and season to taste with salt and pepper.

Heat skillet over medium-high (I use a cast-iron skillet to yield a crisp patty). Add 2 tablespoons oil. Form bean mixture into patties. Working in batches, fry patties 3–4 minutes on each side adding more oil to the skillet as needed. Transfer to paper towel or place in 200°F oven to keep hot. Remove guacamole from refrigerator, discard pits and serve with patties and salsa.

Note: Patties can be made in advance, refrigerated and reheated. Simply wrap in foil and heat in 300°F oven for 10–15 minutes.

MAKES 8 patties

Tofu Salad

THIS SALAD IS SURE TO SATISFY even your meat-eating friends. For a special lunch or light dinner, serve it on a bed of salad greens surrounded by slices of cantaloupe, fresh tomatoes and avocado.

---

24 ounces extra firm silken tofu, cut into ½-inch slices

½ cup Bragg Liquid Aminos

3 tablespoons mirin

2 tablespoons brown rice vinegar

1 cup water

2 stalks celery, diced

½ red onion, diced

1 roasted red pepper, diced

1 cup halved grapes

2 tablespoons chopped fresh parsley

1½ teaspoons dried sage

¼ cup grapeseed oil mayonnaise

Freshly ground black pepper

Preheat oven to 425°F.

Place tofu slices side by side in large glass casserole. In small bowl, whisk together aminos, mirin, vinegar and water and pour over tofu. Marinate 20 minutes, then transfer tofu slices to a lightly oiled cookie sheet and roast 15 minutes. Remove from oven, flip tofu slices and roast another 10 minutes, or until firm throughout and crisp on the outside.

When tofu is cool enough to handle, cut into ½-inch randomly shaped pieces. Place in large bowl and toss with celery, onion, roasted red pepper, grapes, parsley and sage. Fold in mayonnaise, season to taste with pepper and serve room temperature or chilled.

SERVES 4

Tempeh Quesadillas

IF YOU'RE LOOKING FOR SOMETHING to sink your teeth into, this is it. You can find rice tortillas in the freezer section of your natural food store. If you're cutting down on gluten or carbs like bread, these nutritious alternatives make a great treat. They handle best when lightly grilled. Corn tortillas are another nice gluten-free alternative.

4   rice tortillas

1   8-ounce package tempeh

1   cup prepared salsa

1   cup chopped
     romaine lettuce

2   cups shredded rice cheese

Grapeseed oil or extra
     virgin olive oil

Cut tempeh into pieces and steam 5 minutes. Remove from heat and set aside. When cool enough to handle, crumble into large bowl and stir in salsa.

Lightly oil griddle or skillet and place over medium heat. Place 1 tortilla in skillet, sprinkle with ½ cup shredded cheese, top with half of the tempeh, ¼ cup chopped lettuce, ½ cup cheese and another tortilla. Grill 3–4 minutes, carefully flip and grill another 3–4 minutes. Remove from heat. Repeat with remaining tortillas and filling. Slice into wedges and serve.

SERVES 6–8

Pineapple Tempeh Kebabs

THESE KEBABS ARE SWEET AND SAVORY and a great main course for a summer barbeque. Serve them on their own or over basmati or Chinese forbidden black rice. For maximum flavor, leave yourself plenty of time to marinate the tempeh.

KEBABS

2   8-ounce packages tempeh, cut into squares

1   red onion, cut into wedges

2   green bell peppers, cut into triangles

½   fresh pineapple, cut into triangles

MARINADE

¾   cup pineapple juice

2   tablespoons extra virgin olive oil

1   tablespoon tamari

1   tablespoon maple syrup

2   garlic cloves, minced

1   tablespoon grated fresh ginger

1   tablespoon chopped fresh mint

1   tablespoon minced red onion

In medium pot, steam tempeh for 5 minutes. Remove from heat, cool slightly and place squares in large sealable container.

Add onion, green pepper and pineapple to container with tempeh. In small bowl, whisk together all marinade ingredients, pour into container, seal and shake. Refrigerate at least 1 hour, flipping container several times every 15–20 minutes to redistribute marinade.

If using wooden skewers, soak in water for 15 minutes before assembling kebabs. Place ingredients on skewers in an alternating pattern, leaving room to grab ends of skewers.

Heat grill to medium-high and cook kebabs 3–4 minutes per side until cooked through. Remove from heat and serve.

SERVES 4

Quinoa and Black Bean Salad with Apricot Lime Vinaigrette

THIS SALAD HAS A FRUITY TWIST that makes it particularly light and refreshing and provides an interesting change from my more traditional black bean salad. Much of this salad can be prepared in advance, but hold off on adding the tomatoes, seeds or dressing until you're ready to serve.

¾ cup quinoa

1¼ cups water

Pinch of sea salt

3 cups cooked black beans

½ cup chopped red onion

1 mango, peeled, pitted and diced

1 cup peeled and diced jícama

1 cup halved cherry tomatoes

¼ cup toasted sunflower seeds

¼ cup toasted pumpkin seeds

VINAIGRETTE

¼ cup extra virgin olive oil

2 tablespoons lime juice

¼ cup apricot nectar or juice

2 jalapeños, seeded and minced

½ cup chopped fresh mint

Sea salt and freshly ground black pepper

Bring water to boil and add quinoa and salt. Cover, reduce heat and simmer until all water is absorbed (about 15 minutes). Remove from heat and set aside to cool.

Place beans, onion, mango and jícama in large bowl. Fluff cooled quinoa with fork, add to bowl and gently fold to combine.

In small bowl, whisk together all dressing ingredients. Pour dressing over salad and toss to coat. Fold in tomatoes, sunflower seeds and pumpkin seeds just before serving.

SERVES 8

Sprouted Quinoa Tabbouleh

IF YOU LIKE TABBOULEH AS MUCH AS I DO, but can't eat gluten, you no longer have to do without! Don't forget to leave yourself 24 hours to sprout your quinoa before assembling this high-protein, low-fat, non-gluten tabbouleh. I like to start soaking my quinoa at night just before I go to bed, rinse it when I wake up and then assemble my salad just before dinner.

½ cup quinoa

½ cup chopped fresh mint

½ cup chopped fresh parsley

1 cup diced cucumber

1 cup halved cherry tomatoes

2 tablespoons extra virgin olive oil

2 garlic cloves, minced

¼ cup lemon juice

Sea salt

SPROUTING QUINOA

Rinse quinoa thoroughly and place in bowl with enough water to cover. Allow quinoa to absorb water, about 4 hours. Place quinoa in fine-mesh strainer, rinse and place the strainer on plate on counter. Rinse two more times during the day. Quinoa will sprout within 24 hours.

PREPARING SALAD

In large bowl, combine sprouted quinoa with remaining ingredients. Season to taste with sea salt and serve chilled or at room temperature.

SERVES 6

Sprouted Quinoa with Strawberries and Lime

QUINOA IS ONE OF JUST A FEW GRAINS that I find light enough to enjoy in the summer, and sprouting it makes it even more cooling and nutritious. Watermelon radishes, with their vibrant pink flesh, are a sweet and colorful addition to this salad, and they seem to be getting easier to find each year. If you can't get your hands on them, substitute red radishes or make this salad with no radishes at all.

---

1 cup quinoa

½ cup peeled and diced jícama

2 avocados, peeled, pitted and diced

4 apricots (fresh or dried), diced

3 tomatillos, husked and diced

1 cup quartered strawberries

1 yellow bell pepper, diced

½ watermelon radish, peeled and diced

DRESSING

¼ cup extra virgin olive oil

3 tablespoons lime juice

Zest and juice of 1 orange

1 jalapeño, seeded and minced

2 tablespoons chopped fresh cilantro

2 tablespoons fresh mint

Sea salt

SPROUTING QUINOA

Rinse quinoa thoroughly and place in bowl with enough water to cover. Allow quinoa to absorb water, about 4 hours. Place quinoa in fine-mesh strainer, rinse and place the strainer on plate on counter. Rinse 2 times during the day. Quinoa will sprout within 24 hours.

PREPARING SALAD

In large bowl, combine sprouted quinoa, jícama, avocado, apricots, tomatillos, strawberries, yellow pepper and watermelon radish. In separate bowl, whisk together all dressing ingredients. Pour over salad, toss to combine and refrigerate. Serve cold.

SERVES 8

Pesto Pasta Salad

THIS PASTA SALAD HAS BEEN TO MORE FAMILY PICNICS than I can count! Freshly made pesto turns this basic salad into something special. For variety, experiment with lemon basil or even lemon balm instead of traditional basil for another light and wonderful pesto. I've also been known to make a more heart-healthy version with walnuts or pumpkin seeds instead of pine nuts. Experiment freely to discover the combination you like best.

1½ pounds pasta
(fusilli or tortellini)

Extra virgin olive oil

3 cups broccoli florets

4 carrots, sliced into
¼-inch rounds

1 yellow bell pepper, diced

10 cherry tomatoes, halved

1½ cups black olives, pitted

PESTO

3 garlic cloves, peeled

2½ cups fresh basil or
lemon basil leaves

1 cup toasted pine nuts

½ cup soy or rice parmesan
cheese

½ cup extra virgin olive oil

Cook pasta according to directions on package. Drain, rinse, then drain again and return to pot. Drizzle with olive oil and set aside.

PREPARING PESTO

With food processor running, drop in garlic cloves and process until minced. Add remaining pesto ingredients and process until smooth, scrapping down sides of bowl as needed.

PREPARING SALAD

Bring 4 cups of water to boil. Place broccoli florets and carrots in medium bowl. Cover with boiling water and let sit for 1 minute. Drain, rinse with cold water and drain again. Add to pasta along with pepper, tomatoes and olives. Fold in pesto. Serve warm or chilled.

SERVES 8

Wheatberry Salad

THIS SALAD IS A SNAP TO PREPARE and makes a great side dish or main dish for breakfast, lunch or dinner. Wheatberries can be hard to digest, so make sure to take the time to soak them first. For a change, substitute your favorite vinaigrette for the sesame oil and lime juice. To make this salad gluten-free, use wild rice instead of wheatberries.

1½ cups wheatberries

Sea salt

4–5 scallions, chopped

1 cup chopped peaches (apples are a nice substitute in fall)

½ cup currants

¼ cup toasted sunflower seeds

Juice of 1 lime

3 tablespoons toasted sesame oil

Rinse wheatberries, soak in bowl with enough water to cover for at least 1 hour, then drain. In large pot, bring 3¼ cups water to boil. Add wheatberries and pinch of salt, reduce heat, cover, and simmer until all water is absorbed (35–45 minutes). Set aside to cool, then fluff with fork.

In large bowl, combine cooked wheatberries with scallions, peaches, currants and toasted sunflower seeds. Toss with lime juice, toasted sesame oil and pinch of salt. Serve at room temperature or chilled.

SERVES 8

Grilled Polenta with Mushroom Ragoût

POLENTA IS NOT DIFFICULT TO MAKE, but it does require time to cool and firm. To enjoy this dish without the fuss, look for prepared polenta in your natural food store. Either way, this dish is a snap to whip up, and the fresh mushrooms add rich, complex flavor.

POLENTA

5½ cups water

1 teaspoon sea salt

1½ cups polenta

12 sun-dried tomatoes, reconstituted in hot water, drained and chopped

MUSHROOM RAGOÛT

2 tablespoons extra virgin olive oil

2 garlic cloves, peeled

1½ pounds wild mushrooms (shiitake, cremini, portobello and/or mitake varieties)

4 teaspoons chopped fresh marjoram

2 tablespoons chopped fresh parsley

½ cup vegetable stock

1 cup chopped fresh tomatoes

Sea salt and freshly ground black pepper

PREPARING POLENTA

In large sauté pan, bring water to boil over medium-high heat. Add salt. Reduce heat and, whisking continuously, slowly pour in polenta. Add sun-dried tomatoes and stir constantly until polenta is thick and a spoon can stand straight up in it. Pour into 8 x 8-inch square glass baking dish, cool and place in refrigerator to set.

PREPARING RAGOÛT

In large saucepan over medium heat, sauté oil and garlic until fragrant (2–3 minutes). Add mushrooms, marjoram and parsley. Season to taste with salt and pepper and sauté 4–5 minutes. Add vegetable stock and chopped tomatoes and simmer until mushrooms are soft and sauce has started to reduce. Remove from heat, cover and set aside.

FINISHING

Remove polenta from refrigerator and cut into 6 squares. Heat grill pan or griddle over medium-high heat and grill each polenta square 3–4 minutes per side. Place patties on individual plates or serving tray, top with mushroom ragoût and serve.

SERVES 6

Nuts Over Strawberry Rhubarb Pie

OH, THE RECIPES THAT COME TOGETHER when your children are allergic to wheat. This savory and gluten-free crust brings out the tartness of the rhubarb more than a traditional strawberry rhubarb pie, making this quite a favorite in my home.

CRUST

1¼ cups almonds
1¼ cups pecans
1¼ cups walnuts
1 cup brown rice flour
½ cup maple syrup
½ cup canola oil
Pinch of sea salt

FILLING

¾ cup apple juice
2 tablespoons maple syrup
5 stalks rhubarb, cut into 1-inch pieces
4 cups strawberries, de-stemmed and cut into large chunks
3 tablespoons arrowroot or kudzu
1 teaspoon agar powder or flakes

Preheat oven to 350°F.

PREPARING CRUST

Place all nuts in food processor and pulse until mixture resembles coarse meal. Add rice flour, syrup, oil and salt and pulse to combine. Place ⅔ of mixture in lightly oiled 9-inch pie plate, press down to form crust, and bake 15–20 minutes until lightly browned. Remove from oven and set aside on wire rack to cool. Keep the oven on.

PREPARING FILLING

Combine apple juice and maple syrup in large pot over medium heat, bring to boil and reduce to simmer. Slowly whisk in arrowroot and agar. Cook 2 minutes or until juice thickens. Add rhubarb and strawberries and cook until rhubarb just starts to fall apart. Remove from heat and cool 2–3 minutes.

FINISHING

Pour filling into prepared pie crust and sprinkle with remaining nut mixture. Place in oven and bake 40 minutes. Remove from oven and set aside for 5–10 minutes to set. Serve warm.

Fresh Fruit Tart with Almond Crust

AN ELEGANT, EASY AND HEALTHY PRESENTATION for summer fruit and berries.

CRUST

1 cup almonds
1 cup rolled oats
½ cup oat bran
Pinch of sea salt
3 tablespoons maple syrup
3 tablespoons canola oil
1 teaspoon almond extract

FILLING

4 kiwis, peeled and thinly sliced
3 peaches, thinly sliced
3 cups berries of choice
1 cup apple juice
¼ cup fruit nectar or juice of choice
2 tablespoons maple syrup
1 tablespoon agar powder or flakes
1 tablespoon arrowroot or kudzu
1 teaspoon vanilla extract

PREPARING CRUST

Preheat oven to 350°F.

Place nuts in food processor and pulse to chop coarsely. Add rolled oats, oat bran and salt and process until mixture resembles coarse meal. In small bowl, whisk together maple syrup, oil and almond extract. Add to almond-oat mixture and process to combine. Transfer to 9-inch oiled tart pan or springform pan and press down to form crust. Pierce several times with fork and bake 15 minutes or until lightly browned. Remove from oven and set aside on wire rack to cool.

ASSEMBLING TART

Arrange sliced kiwis and peaches around outside edge of tart and fill center with berries. In medium pot over no heat, combine apple juice, fruit nectar, syrup, agar and arrowroot. Turn heat to medium-high and whisk continuously until agar dissolves and mixture thickens. Add vanilla, remove from heat and set aside to cool 5 minutes. Spoon evenly over tart and refrigerate at least 1 hour before serving.

Strawberry Custard with Fresh Berries and Lemon Peel

THIS SWEET AND REFRESHING DESSERT is the perfect choice after your annual strawberry-picking outing. Substitute white rice flour or ivory teff flour for the all-purpose flour for an equally delicious gluten-free version.

2	pounds fresh strawberries, de-stemmed
24	ounces firm silken tofu
½	teaspoon vanilla extract
⅔	cup maple syrup
⅓	cup all-purpose unbleached white flour
1	cup mixed berries
2	tablespoons lemon peel

Purée strawberries in food processor and press through a fine sieve into separate bowl. Discard seeds and set liquid aside.

Clean food processor and whip tofu until creamy (make sure all chunks get whipped). Add vanilla, syrup, strawberry liquid and flour. Process to combine. Pour into serving bowl or individual parfait or martini glasses. Refrigerate at least 1 hour. Top with mixed berries and lemon peel. Serve cold.

SERVES 8

Peach, Fresh Fig and Bourbon Crisp with Pecan Topping

THIS TOPPING CAN BE PRESSED INTO A PIE SHELL or crumbled over fruit for a quick and delicious dessert as I've done here. If fresh figs aren't available, either leave them out or turn this into a completely new dessert by using berries and no bourbon. The skins of organic peaches add nice texture and color.

FILLING

8–10	peaches, pitted and cut into wedges
6–8	fresh figs, cut into wedges
2	tablespoons agave nectar
1	teaspoon vanilla extract
3	tablespoons bourbon
3	tablespoons brown rice flour

Pinch of sea salt

TOPPING

4	cups pecans
½	cup brown rice flour or ivory teff flour
⅓	cup canola oil
¼	cup agave nectar

Pinch of sea salt

Preheat oven to 350°F.

PREPARING FILLING

Place peaches and figs in large bowl. In separate bowl, combine agave nectar, vanilla and bourbon. Pour over fruit, sprinkle with flour and salt and gently fold to combine. Transfer to casserole and set aside.

PREPARING TOPPING

Chop nuts in food processor until mixture resembles coarse meal. Add flour and process to combine. Add oil, agave nectar and salt. Process until mixture is moist enough to stick together when pressed, but still crumbly.

FINISHING

Spread nut mixture evenly over peaches, cover loosely with foil and bake 30 minutes. Remove foil and bake another 20 minutes or until peaches are soft. Remove from oven, cool slightly and serve warm.

Strawberry Rhubarb Compote with Cashew Cream

THERE'S SOMETHING ABOUT FRESHLY PICKED RHUBARB at the farm stand that I simply can't pass up. This may be one of the simplest ways to use rhubarb, and the finished product is a smooth and sweet complement to this rich cashew cream. For an even quicker dessert, serve the compote over chocolate or vanilla ice cream.

CASHEW CREAM

- 2 cups apple juice
- 2 cups lightly roasted cashews
- 3 tablespoons maple syrup

COMPOTE

- 2 cups chopped rhubarb
- ½ cup apple juice
- 3 tablespoons arrowroot or kudzu
- 1 teaspoon agar powder
- 4 cups de-stemmed and halved strawberries
- Fresh mint or lemon balm sprigs for garnish

PREPARING CASHEW CREAM

In small pot, bring apple juice to boil and remove from heat. Place cashews and syrup in food processor. You may not need all of the juice so turn on machine and slowly add juice to cashews and syrup until you achieve the desired texture. Refrigerate for 1 hour.

PREPARING COMPOTE

In saucepan over medium heat, combine rhubarb and apple juice and simmer until rhubarb starts to fall apart. Add arrowroot and agar and whisk until mixture starts to thicken. Add strawberries and remove from heat. Set aside to cool slightly.

ASSEMBLING

Layer compote and cashew cream in glasses or glass bowl. Top with sprigs of fresh mint or lemon balm and serve.

SERVES 6

Lemon Berry Cream Pie

I WAS ABSOLUTELY OBSESSED WITH CREATING THIS PIE! I could taste exactly what I was craving, but simply couldn't achieve it. After far too many attempts, it finally came together as I hoped it would and it has been my all-time favorite summer pie ever since. It's creamy, sweet, tart and refreshing and the use of store-bought lemon snaps allows the crust to come together in no time. I hope you love it as much as I do.

CRUST

2	heaping cups lemon snaps
¼	cup canola oil
¼	cup maple syrup

FILLING

1	cup apple juice
¼	cup lemon juice
1	tablespoon agar powder
2½	tablespoons arrowroot
12	ounces extra firm silken tofu
¾	cup maple syrup
2	tablespoons lemon extract
1	tablespoon lemon zest
1	tablespoon vanilla extract

Pinch of sea salt

2–3 cups fresh blueberries

PREPARING CRUST

Preheat oven to 350°F.

Place lemon snaps in food processor and process until they resemble coarse flour. Add oil and syrup and process to combine. Place in 9-inch pie plate and press down to form crust. Bake 12 minutes, then remove from oven, press down any bubbles with the back of a wooden spoon and set aside on wire rack to cool.

PREPARING FILLING

In small pot over no heat, whisk together apple juice, lemon juice, agar powder and arrowroot until there are no lumps. Place over medium heat and stir continuously until mixture thickens and starts to look translucent. Remove from heat and set aside to cool.

In food processor, whip tofu until smooth. Add maple syrup, lemon extract and zest, vanilla and salt, and process briefly. Add apple juice mixture and pulse to just combine.

FINISHING

Pour tofu mixture into pie shell and completely cover top of pie with berries. Refrigerate to chill and set at least 2 hours before serving.

Chocolate Pudding with Fresh Berries

THIS PUDDING IS ONE OF MY MOST USEFUL dessert recipes. I serve it as a pudding; I take out the bananas and use it to frost cakes; and sometimes I take out the bananas, add roasted nuts and pour it into a pie crust for chocolate cream pie.

---

25 ounces extra firm or firm silken tofu

1 teaspoon vanilla extract

Pinch of sea salt

2–3 ripe bananas

1 cup semisweet dark chocolate chips

2 cups strawberries, raspberries and/or blackberries

Wrap blocks of tofu in towels and press to remove excess liquid. In food processor, blend tofu, vanilla and salt. Scrape sides of bowl and blend again until there are no lumps. Add bananas and blend until smooth.

In small saucepan, melt chocolate, immediately add to tofu mixture and process until combined. Pour mixture into large serving bowl or individual parfait glasses and refrigerate at least 1 hour to firm and chill. Remove from refrigerator, top with fresh berries and serve.

SERVES 6

Mixed Berry Tart

SIMPLE, ELEGANT, GLUTEN-FREE, LOW CALORIE AND SATISFYING.
Who could ask for more?

CRUST

1½ cups ivory teff flour
¼ teaspoon sea salt
½ cup maple syrup
¼ cup canola oil

FILLING

5 cups fresh mixed berries
1½ cups clear apple juice
2 tablespoons maple syrup
1 tablespoon agar powder or flakes
2 tablespoons arrowroot
1 teaspoon vanilla extract

PREPARING CRUST

Preheat oven to 350°F.

Place flour, salt, syrup and oil in food processor and pulse to combine. Pour mixture into 9-inch oiled tart or springform pan. Press down to form crust. Pierce several times with fork and bake 15 minutes until lightly browned. Remove from oven and set aside on wire rack to cool.

ASSEMBLING TART

Fill tart with berries. In medium pot over medium-high heat, combine apple juice, syrup and agar. Whisk continuously until agar dissolves. Slowly sprinkle in arrowroot and continue whisking until mixture thickens and no clumps remain. Add vanilla, remove from heat and set aside to cool 5 minutes. Spoon evenly over tart and refrigerate 1 hour or until set.

Fresh Berries with Tofu Cream

THERE ARE A FEW BASIC RECIPES that are not only delicious on their own, but also helpful for making a variety of other recipes. This tofu cream is one of them. You can serve it on top of fresh berries, top it with granola for dipping sliced fruit, spread it between two layers of cake or serve it over pie. No matter how you use it, you just can't go wrong!

3   cups fresh berries
     of choice
Mint leaves for garnish

TOFU CREAM
18   ounces extra firm
     silken tofu
¼   cup apple juice
¼   cup cashew butter
⅓   cup maple syrup
1   teaspoon vanilla extract
Pinch of sea salt
2   teaspoons arrowroot
3   tablespoons rice milk

Drain tofu, wrap in towels and press out excess water. Place in food processor and whip until perfectly smooth, scraping down sides of bowl so that all pieces get whipped. Add apple juice, cashew butter, maple syrup, vanilla and sea salt and process until smooth.

Combine rice milk and arrowroot in small pot. Place over medium heat and whisk continuously until thick (3–4 minutes). Remove from heat, add to tofu and process to combine.

Transfer tofu cream to bowl and refrigerate 1 hour or until cold. Divide berries, place in individual bowls and top with tofu cream and mint leaves.

SERVES 6

Autumn is a second spring when every leaf is a flower.

ALBERT CAMUS

Fall

It's hard to say good-bye to summer's bright and colorful palette, but by mid-September I am ready for cool crisp mornings, apple-picking excursions, pumpkin carving and hayrides. A colorful blanket of foliage drapes over New England. Farms sell bunches of fresh herbs for drying, bags of basil for making pesto, boxes of tomatoes for canning and gourds for decorating. Apples and pears come in reds, yellows and greens, reflecting the changing leaves around them, and the winter squash are so tasty that my children devour them, skin and all. There's nothing like the sweetness of kale and collard greens after fall's first frost. While most of my family reserve dark leafy greens for dinner, these greens are often my breakfast of choice. I enjoy starting my day with their uplifting, long-lasting energy. It's a great way to keep positive and balanced while transitioning into the darker, colder months ahead.

FALL

Spiced Kukicha Iced Tea

KUKICHA TEA IS HIGHLY REGARDED for its medicinal properties. It is alkalinizing and strengthening to the body and can be consumed daily. It also has almost no caffeine, supports healthy digestion and can be helpful in treating heart disease and fatigue. Kukicha is even safe for children. You can drink it straight or with a dash of lemon juice and agave nectar, but this recipe gives you a way to create a medicine you'll love to take. Choose any combination of fruit juices to make it your own.

4   cups water

4   1-ounce kukicha
     tea bags

1   cinnamon stick

¾   cup orange juice
     (preferably freshly
     squeezed)

2   cups apple cider

1   cup pomegranate juice

Fresh sprigs of mint or lemon
     balm for garnish

Bring water to boil and remove from heat. Add tea bags and cinnamon stick and steep 10 minutes. With slotted spoon, remove and discard cinnamon stick and tea bags. Stir in remaining juices and refrigerate to chill. Serve with sprigs of fresh mint or lemon balm.

MAKES 7 cups

Ginger Pear Sauce

THIS IS A WONDERFUL ALTERNATIVE to applesauce and provides a nice balance and pleasant surprise when served with Seitan Walnut Stuffed Collard Greens *(page 181)* or Three Sisters Deep-Dish Pie *(page 168)*.

---

10 ripe pears

8 cloves

2 tablespoons grated fresh ginger

2 cups water or pear juice

1 cinnamon stick

Peel, core and slice pears and place in large pot with cloves, ginger, water or pear juice and cinnamon stick. Bring to boil over medium-high heat, cover, reduce heat and simmer 6–8 minutes until fruit is soft. Remove from heat and let cool slightly. Discard cinnamon stick and then purée fruit with handheld blender. Serve warm or at room temperature.

MAKES 3 cups

Cranberry Chutney

AS A CHILD, I INSISTED ON STORE-BOUGHT CRANBERRY SAUCE – no chunks, just that smooth roll, complete with indentations from the can. When I finally tasted my mother's homemade chutney, I was converted. I now make it in huge batches, give it as gifts around the holidays and even freeze it to have throughout the year. It goes great on a turkey sandwich with avocado and honey mustard or with vegetable pot pie. Once you taste it, you'll understand why I'm addicted.

2	cups fresh cranberries
1	cup raisins
½	cup sucanat
½	cup maple syrup
1	tablespoon ground cinnamon
2	teaspoons grated fresh ginger
¼	teaspoon ground cloves
1	cup water
1	small onion, chopped
3	medium apples, cored and chopped
4	stalks celery, chopped
1	teaspoon grated lemon peel

Combine cranberries, raisins, sucanat, maple syrup, cinnamon, ginger, cloves and water in Dutch oven. Place over medium heat and cook 15 minutes. Stir in onion, apples and celery and cook 15 minutes more. Remove from heat, fold in lemon peel, and serve.

Chutney can be made in advance and stored in an airtight container in the freezer.

MAKES 4 cups

Apple Chutney

THANKSGIVING WOULDN'T BE THE SAME without cranberry chutney, but sometimes I crave a more delicate condiment – something between Mom's cranberry variety and my homemade applesauce. This recipe fills that gap perfectly and also makes a great accompaniment to Three Sisters Deep-Dish Pie *(page 168)*.

---

1   cup apple cider or juice
2   cinnamon sticks
5   cloves
8   large firm and tart apples (Granny Smith, Macoun or other)
1   cup golden raisins
½   cup maple syrup
1   tablespoon grated fresh ginger
1   large onion, diced
1   fennel bulb, halved, cored and diced
Pinch of sea salt
Zest of 1 lemon

Place apple cider, cinnamon sticks and cloves in small pot over medium heat and simmer 15 minutes. Turn off heat, remove cinnamon sticks and cloves and set aside. Meanwhile, peel, core and dice apples.

In 2-quart pot, combine apples, raisins, maple syrup, ginger, onion, fennel and salt. Place over medium-high heat and add in spiced apple cider. Bring to boil, reduce heat and simmer 45 minutes or until chutney is thick. Remove from heat, fold in lemon zest and serve warm or cold.

MAKES 3 cups

Herbed White Bean Dip

THIS DIP CAN BE MADE IN ADVANCE and stored in an airtight container in the refrigerator, but the flavors will be their best at room temperature or slightly heated. Serve with Garlic Crostini *(page 204)*, Pita Chips *(page 261)*, crudités or in a sandwich with baby field greens and sliced tomato.

---

2   tablespoons extra virgin olive oil

2   garlic cloves, minced

2   shallots or 1 small sweet onion, diced

2   tablespoons mirin

1   tablespoon minced fresh rosemary

1   tablespoon fresh thyme or lemon thyme leaves

¼   teaspoon sea salt

2   cups cooked white beans (navy, great northern or cannellini)

4–5 dashes hot pepper sauce

In small skillet over medium heat, sauté garlic and shallots in olive oil until soft (about 3 minutes). Add mirin, rosemary, thyme and salt and reduce heat to medium-low. Cook for 5 minutes, then remove from heat.

In large bowl, combine beans with sautéed shallot mixture. Purée with handheld blender. Season to taste with hot pepper sauce and serve at room temperature.

MAKES 1½ cups

Lentil Walnut Pâté

THIS DIP REMINDS ME of the chopped liver my mother used to make when I was a child, only better. While it works without the walnuts, they add richness and complexity that's well worth the extra fuss. Serve with Pita Chips *(page 261)*, thin rye bread rounds or crackers.

1   cup brown or
    green lentils
1   thumb-size piece kombu
2   cups water
1   tablespoon extra
    virgin olive oil
2   onions, chopped
1   cup walnut pieces
Ume plum vinegar
Water and/or extra virgin
    olive oil

Preheat oven to 300°F.

Rinse lentils and place in pot or rice cooker with kombu and water. Cover and bring to boil over high heat. Reduce heat to simmer and cook 35–40 minutes until water is absorbed. Remove from heat, discard kombu and set lentils aside.

While lentils are cooking, crush or chop walnuts and roast on a parchment-lined cookie sheet for 12 minutes or until golden brown. In medium skillet over medium heat, sauté onion in olive oil until translucent (about 5 minutes).

Place cooked lentils in food processor with roasted walnuts, sautéed onions and a few dashes of vinegar. Add water and/or olive oil a tablespoon at a time and process untl smooth. Season to taste with vinegar and serve at room temperature or cold.

MAKES 3 cups

Apple Squash Soup

THIS SWEET, SILKY AND UPLIFTING DISH is the quintessential fall soup. I serve it to friends and family and even send it to school for my children's lunches. Pair it with a salad or some sautéed greens and grains for an easy and satisfying meal.

1	large butternut squash
1	large yellow onion, chopped
2	tablespoons grapeseed oil
4	large apples, peeled, cored and quartered
4	cups vegetable stock
1	cup rice milk
¼	cup coconut milk
½	teaspoon ground nutmeg

Sea salt

Peel squash, cut in half and remove seeds. Cut into 2-inch pieces.

In large pot over medium heat, sauté onion in oil until soft (about 5 minutes). Add squash, apples, stock, rice milk, coconut milk and nutmeg. Cover, bring to boil, then reduce heat and simmer 20 minutes or until squash is soft. Purée with handheld blender and remove from heat to cool slightly. Season to taste with salt and serve.

SERVES 6

Autumn Harvest Soup

THIS AUTUMN SOUP IS A NUTRITIONAL POWERHOUSE. With shiitake mushroom stock to help reduce blood cholesterol levels, dark leafy greens rich in calcium and legumes to regulate your blood sugar, support your thyroid and balance your hormones, this meal in a pot is just what the doctor ordered! For those with a bigger appetite, serve over soba noodles or brown rice.

---

4 dried shiitake mushrooms

6 cups water

2 tablespoons extra virgin olive oil

1 large onion, diced

3 garlic cloves, minced

1 tablespoon grated fresh ginger

3 carrots, diced

4 cups chopped kale or collard greens

2 cups cooked cannellini beans

¼ cup mirin

Splash of tamari

Splash of apple cider vinegar

4–5 dashes toasted sesame oil

Freshly ground black pepper

Place dried mushrooms in medium pot with 6 cups water. Bring to boil, then reduce heat and simmer 15 minutes. Remove from heat and set aside to cool slightly. When mushrooms are soft, remove from broth and cut off and discard stems. Dice caps and place back in pot with broth.

In large pot over medium heat, sauté onion, garlic and ginger in oil 3 minutes. Add carrots and sauté 3 minutes. Add kale or collard greens, beans and mirin and sauté until greens are deep green and tender. Pour broth and mushrooms into pot with kale, add tamari and vinegar and simmer 5–7 minutes. Season to taste with toasted sesame oil and black pepper and serve.

SERVES 6

Carrot Ginger Soup

THIS NONDAIRY SOUP IS SURPRISINGLY EASY TO MAKE and is big on taste. A handheld blender is perfect for puréeing soups and requires less cleanup than a food processor. When possible, prepare soups a day in advance to allow the flavors to blend. Then simply reheat, garnish and serve.

2	tablespoons grapeseed oil
1	onion, chopped
1	tablespoon grated fresh ginger
4	cups chopped carrots
½	cup rolled oats
½	cup orange juice (preferably freshly squeezed)

Water or vegetable stock

3	tablespoons mellow white miso

Chopped fresh parsley for garnish

In large pot over medium heat, sauté onion and ginger in oil 3 minutes. Add carrots, oats, orange juice and enough water or stock to just cover carrots. Bring to boil, reduce heat, cover and let simmer until carrots are soft (about 20 minutes). Turn off heat and purée with handheld blender. In small bowl, dissolve miso in ½ cup room-temperature water and stir into soup. Garnish with parsley and serve.

SERVES 4

Creamy Shiitake and Chickpea Soup

LEGUMES ARE HIGH IN PROTEIN and are perfect for making satisfying soups. Chickpeas in particular are a great source of iron, calcium and heart-healthy unsaturated fats. Combined with dried shiitake mushrooms (known for their cholesterol-lowering properties) and calcium-rich broccoli, this soup is as healing as it is delicious.

---

4   dried shiitake mushrooms

1   large strip kombu

2   cups water

1   medium onion, chopped

1   garlic clove, minced

1   tablespoon extra virgin olive oil

3   tablespoons lemon juice

2   tablespoons tamari

3   cups cooked chickpeas

1   tablespoon kudzu or arrowroot powder

2   cups broccoli cut into bite-size pieces

⅓   cup raisins

Sea salt and freshly ground black pepper

Soak dried mushrooms and kombu for 30 minutes in bowl with enough water to cover. Saving the soaking liquid, remove mushrooms and kombu. Discard mushroom stems and thinly slice caps. Mince kombu and return both sliced caps and kombu to soaking liquid.

In large pot over medium heat, sauté onion and garlic in oil for 3 minutes. Add lemon juice, tamari, chickpeas, mushrooms, kombu and soaking water and stir. Dissolve kudzu in ¼ cup water and stir into soup. Cover and simmer 15 minutes.

Meanwhile, place broccoli in bowl and pour in enough boiling water to cover. Let sit for 2 minutes, then drain and set aside.

Using handheld blender, lightly purée soup. Add raisins and cook 3 minutes or until soft. Add broccoli and simmer briefly to heat through. Season to taste with salt and pepper and serve.

SERVES 4

Savory Black Bean Soup

I LOVE BLACK BEANS YEAR ROUND, whether in salads, burritos, chili or this favorite soup. For a simple fall meal, serve with corn chips and a dollop of Tofu Sour Cream *(page 101)*.

1	thumb-size piece kombu
1	tablespoon extra virgin olive oil
4	garlic cloves, minced
1	onion, chopped
1	stalk celery, chopped
2	carrots, chopped
1	teaspoon ground cumin
¼	teaspoon cayenne pepper
¼	teaspoon sea salt
6	cups cooked black beans
4	cups water or vegetable stock
1	cup diced tomatoes (preferably without skins)
2	tablespoons mirin
1	tablespoon tamari

Chopped fresh cilantro for garnish

Place kombu in bowl with enough warm water to cover and soak 10 minutes or until soft. Drain, mince kombu and set aside.

In large pot over medium heat, sauté garlic and onion in oil 3 minutes. Add celery, carrots, cumin, cayenne and salt. Sauté 8 minutes or until carrots are tender.

Add beans to pot along with water or stock, kombu, tomatoes, mirin and tamari. Bring to simmer and cook 30 minutes to combine flavors. For a creamier texture, purée some of the soup with handheld blender. Garnish with cilantro and serve.

SERVES 8

Marinated Bitter Greens

THIS GREEN LEAF SALAD MARINATES in its dressing just long enough to slightly wilt the greens, making them less bitter and easier to digest. The acidity of the apple cider vinegar helps this process and adds the perfect complement to Fall's sweet squashes and fruits. For an extra-special touch, garnish with pomegranate seeds.

4   cups chopped fall salad greens (try watercress, endive, radicchio and romaine lettuce)

MARINADE

1   shallot, minced

2   tablespoons apple cider vinegar

4   teaspoons brown rice syrup

2   teaspoons maple or honey mustard

½   teaspoon Bragg Liquid Aminos

3   tablespoons toasted sesame oil

¼   cup canola oil

Place mixed greens in large bowl. Whisk together marinade ingredients either by hand or with handheld blender. Pour marinade over greens, toss to coat and set aside 10 minutes. Toss again, transfer greens to salad bowl or individual plates and serve.

SERVES 4

Quick Boiled Broccoli and Stems with Toasted Sesame Seeds

I CAN BE COMPLETELY SATISFIED with a bowl of quinoa topped with this simple broccoli dish. Even when I serve it to company, people exclaim that they've never tasted such delicious broccoli! Sometimes simpler truly is better.

---

1   bunch broccoli
2   tablespoons flax seed oil
1   teaspoon ume plum vinegar
2   tablespoons toasted sesame seeds

Cut broccoli florets from stems. Chop florets into pieces and place in pot. Trim and discard dry ends from broccoli stems. Peel, discard outer skins, chop stems and add to pot with florets. Add 2 inches of water, cover, bring to boil and cook 2–3 minutes or until bright green and just tender. Drain water and toss broccoli with flax seed oil and vinegar. Sprinkle with sesame seeds and serve.

SERVES 4

Warm Greens with Citrus Dressing and Pomegranate

USING POMEGRANATE SEEDS IS A SPECIAL WAY to dress up a variety of dishes. Combining greens with this citrus dressing, you simply can't go wrong, and the addition of pomegranate seeds on top is like icing on the cake!

---

2 bunches greens
(try bok choy, kale or
collard greens)

1 bunch watercress

Seeds from ½ large
pomegranate

DRESSING

Juice of 1 orange

2 tablespoons brown
rice syrup

2 tablespoons extra
virgin olive oil

½ teaspoon grated
fresh ginger

1 tablespoon mirin

1 tablespoon tamari

1 tablespoon apple cider
vinegar

In small bowl, whisk together all dressing ingredients.

Prepare greens by trimming and discarding dried ends. Cut leaves into bite-size pieces. Keeping watercress aside, place all other greens in large sauté pan. Add citrus dressing and sauté 2 minutes or until bright green and tender. Fold in watercress and cook 1 more minute. Remove from heat and serve topped with pomegranate seeds.

SERVES 4–6

Kale with Caramelized Shallots

KALE COMES IN MANY VARIETIES. My favorite is lacinato (also known as dinosaur kale), but you can use all of the varieties interchangeably. This preparation makes it easy to benefit from kale's vitamins, minerals and chlorophyll. Submerging the whole leaves in boiling water not only saves you the effort of washing, but allows the kale to retain more of its nutrients.

---

2 bunches kale
6 large shallots, thinly sliced
3 tablespoons extra virgin olive oil
1 tablespoon lemon juice
⅛ teaspoon coarse sea salt
Freshly ground black pepper

In large skillet or Dutch oven over medium heat, sauté shallots in 1 tablespoon olive oil for 6–8 minutes or until very soft and caramelized. Add lemon juice and sauté another 2–3 minutes to brown. Remove from heat and set aside.

Bring large pot of water to boil. Cut and remove dried stem ends from kale and submerge whole leaves in boiling water for 2–3 minutes or until tender and bright green. Remove from heat, drain water and cut leaves into bite-size pieces. Add kale to pan with shallots and sauté 1 minute. Add remaining 2 tablespoons oil, season to taste with salt and pepper and serve.

SERVES 6

Kale with Pine Nuts and Currants

KALE IS A NUTRITIONAL POWERHOUSE, but the addition of pine nuts in this recipe makes it more like an indulgence. For a complete meal, serve this dish with wild rice *(page 14)* and Seitan Bourguignon *(page 239)*.

⅓ cup currants

2 tablespoons extra virgin olive oil

2 garlic cloves, minced

½ red onion, diced

2 large bunches kale, chopped

4 dashes ume plum vinegar

¼ cup toasted pine nuts

Plump currants by placing in small pot with ¼ inch water. Bring to boil, then reduce heat and simmer uncovered 3–4 minutes. Remove from heat and set aside.

In large pan over medium heat, sauté garlic and onion in oil until soft (about 3 minutes). Add kale and sauté until tender (4–6 minutes). Add 1–2 tablespoons water as needed to prevent sticking. Drain currants and add to kale. Toss with vinegar, top with toasted pine nuts and serve.

SERVES 6

Tamari-Braised Mustard Greens

MUSTARD GREENS HAVE A BITE SIMILAR TO ARUGULA and can be eaten raw in salads or cooked as in this recipe. These bitter greens are particularly good cleansers and are a rich source of antioxidants. If their bitterness is too much for you, add some kale to your sauté or enjoy them raw and mixed with romaine lettuce in a salad.

---

2   bunches mustard greens
2   tablespoons grapeseed oil
2   garlic cloves, minced
2   tablespoons tamari
2   tablespoons mirin
1   tablespoon gomasio

Trim and discard tough ends of mustard greens. Cut leaves into bite-size pieces and set aside.

In large skillet over medium-low heat, sauté garlic in oil 2 minutes or until soft. Increase heat to medium and add greens, tamari and mirin. Stir to combine, cover and simmer 5 minutes or until greens are tender. Uncover, increase heat to medium-high and cook until liquid has been reduced. Remove from heat, sprinkle with gomasio and serve hot.

SERVES 6

Rutabaga Purée with Orange and Ginger

THIS SWEET AND TANGY RUTABAGA purée makes a light, colorful and delicious change from potatoes or grains. The sweetness of this dish pairs nicely with bitter greens like Brussels sprouts or collard greens.

4–5 large rutabagas
1 tablespoon grated fresh ginger
1 cup orange juice
½ cup water
Sea salt

Peel and chop rutabagas. Place in large pot with ginger, orange juice and water. Cover, bring to boil, then reduce heat and simmer until soft throughout, adding water a little at a time as needed to prevent burning. When soft, remove from heat and pour remaining liquid into separate bowl. Purée rutabagas with handheld blender, adding cooking liquid if needed to achieve desired texture. Season to taste with salt and serve.

SERVES 4

Curried Parsnips

THESE WHIPPED PARSNIPS ARE DELICIOUS AS IS, or they can easily be turned into a smooth and silky soup. Just add 2 cups of vegetable stock after browning the parsnips, bring to a boil and purée.

---

2   pounds parsnips, peeled and thinly sliced

1   tablespoon extra virgin olive oil

1   large leek, quartered and thinly sliced

1   tablespoon grated fresh ginger

1   garlic clove, minced

1   tablespoon mirin

1   teaspoon curry powder

Sea salt

Chopped fresh parsley for garnish

Steam sliced parsnips until not quite tender (time will vary depending on how thick you've sliced your parsnips). Remove from heat and set aside.

In large pan over medium heat, sauté leek, ginger, garlic and mirin in oil until leeks are tender. Add curry powder and parsnips and sauté until parsnips start to brown. Deglaze pan with a little water, releasing any browned bits from the bottom of the pan. Season to taste with salt, top with chopped parsley and serve.

SERVES 4

Roasted Root Vegetables with Truffle Oil

I HAVE A TENDENCY TO EAT THE SAME VEGETABLES for weeks at a time, so every now and again I shop with the intention of buying only vegetables I haven't cooked recently, and that's how this recipe came to be. It usually disappears as soon as I make it, but on the rare occasion that I have some left over, I like to reheat it with cannellini beans or toss it with fresh watercress for a cooler, more cleansing combination.

---

12 Brussels sprouts

1 large rutabaga, peeled and diced

1 fennel bulb, halved and sliced into strips

1 daikon, peeled and diced

1 large onion, cut into wedges or 6 cipollini onions, peeled and halved

8 garlic cloves, peeled

2–3 tablespoons extra virgin olive oil

2 tablespoons balsamic vinegar

2 teaspoons coarse sea salt

White truffle oil

Chopped fresh tarragon

Preheat oven to 425°F.

Prepare Brussels sprouts by trimming off dry ends, peeling away any damaged leaves and cutting in half.

Place vegetables in large bowl and toss with oil, vinegar and salt. Put into 2 glass roasting dishes and roast for 45 minutes or until caramelized. Toss vegetables every 10–15 minutes to prevent burning and encourage even browning. Remove from heat, drizzle with truffle oil, toss with fresh tarragon and serve.

SERVES 4

Spiced Sweet Potato Fries

ONE WAY TO WARD OFF CRAVINGS FOR non-nutritional sweets is to add more naturally sweet foods to your diet. Winter roots and squash offer that welcome addition to any meal, and cutting sweet potatoes into fries allows them to cook up in a snap. They also make delicious leftovers.

3–4 sweet potatoes or yams
1 tablespoon extra virgin olive oil
1 tablespoon balsamic vinegar
1 tablespoon maple syrup
2 teaspoons cinnamon
Coarse sea salt

Preheat oven to 400°F.

Wash potatoes and remove blemish spots and dried ends. Slice into sticks and place in large bowl. Drizzle on remaining ingredients and toss to distribute evenly. Spread coated potatoes in single layer on cookie sheet and bake 10 minutes. Remove from oven, flip slices and bake another 10–20 minutes or until tender and browned. Cooking time will vary depending on thickness of potato slices. Serve hot.

SERVES 6

Root Veggie Fries

THESE ARE FAR FROM ORDINARY FRENCH FRIES! Use a variety of root vegetables for a colorful and sweet side dish that's rich in vitamins and nutrients. I like to double this recipe so I have leftovers to snack on the next day.

1	rutabaga, peeled
4	carrots
4	parsnips, peeled
3	tablespoons extra virgin olive oil
¼	cup yellow cornmeal
1	teaspoon coarse sea salt
½	teaspoon ground nutmeg
Cayenne pepper	

Set oven to broil.

Cut vegetables into sticks and steam 3–4 minutes or until just tender. Remove from heat and place in large bowl. Coat with oil and toss with cornmeal, salt, nutmeg and cayenne. Lightly oil cookie sheet and spread fries in single layer. Broil 3 minutes, then remove from oven, flip fries and broil another 3 minutes or until lightly browned. Serve hot.

SERVES 4

Three Sisters Deep-Dish Pie

THIS LIGHT AND EASY MEAL IN A POT requires just a little advance planning to roast the squash. The rest comes together quickly. Serve with Cranberry Chutney *(page 148)*, Apple Chutney *(page 149)* or Cranberry Applesauce *(page 205)* for a perfect finish.

---

2   medium delicata squash

2   tablespoons extra virgin olive oil

1   large onion, diced

3   carrots, peeled and diced

3   stalks celery, diced

2   tablespoons mirin

½   pound green beans, trimmed

1½ cups corn, fresh or frozen

¾   cup water

2   tablespoons Bragg Liquid Aminos

2   tablespoons arrowroot

Freshly ground black pepper

1   frozen 9-inch pie crust, defrosted

Preheat oven to 400°F.

ROASTING SQUASH

Wash squash well, cut in half lengthwise, remove seeds and rub each section with oil. Place cut side down on cookie sheet or in glass baking dish and roast 25 minutes or until soft throughout. Remove from heat and set aside.

PREPARING FILLING

In Dutch oven or large pot over medium heat, sauté onion in olive oil until soft (about 3 minutes). Add carrots, celery and mirin and sauté 3 minutes. Cut green beans into bite-size pieces, add to pot along with corn and sauté 5 minutes or until beans start to soften. Chop squash into bite-size pieces and fold into mixture.

In small bowl, whisk together water, liquid aminos and arrowroot until smooth. Pour into pot with vegetables and stir until liquid starts to thicken. Season to taste with pepper. Remove from heat and transfer to deep casserole.

FINISHING

Crumble pie crust over top of casserole and cover with foil. Bake 30 minutes. Remove foil and bake 8 minutes longer or until top is lightly browned. Remove from oven and serve.

SERVES 6

Roasted Squash with Fennel and Asparagus

ROASTING SQUASH BRINGS OUT ITS NATURAL SUGARS and blends the flavors of these vegetables beautifully. The slight bitterness of asparagus is a nice complement to these otherwise sweet vegetables and adds an always welcome splash of green. I like to serve this dish over pan-roasted millet.

---

1 large butternut squash, peeled, seeded and diced

1 large fennel bulb, halved, cored and thinly sliced

5 shallots, quartered

5 garlic cloves, peeled

1 pound of asparagus, cut into 2-inch lengths

2 tablespoons extra virgin olive oil

2 teaspoons balsamic vinegar

½ teaspoon coarse sea salt

2 pinches red pepper flakes

Chopped fresh parsley for garnish

Preheat oven to 400°F.

In large bowl, combine squash, fennel, shallots and garlic. Add oil, vinegar, salt and pepper flakes and toss to coat evenly. Spread vegetables on cookie sheet and roast 20 minutes. Remove from oven, fold in asparagus and return to oven for another 20 minutes or until all vegetables are tender. Garnish with parsley and serve.

SERVES 6

Savory Stuffed Pumpkins

TRY THIS RECIPE STUFFED in individual sweet pumpkins, delicata squash or acorn squash. For an even more dramatic presentation, clean out, roast and stuff a large hubbard squash. To make this recipe gluten-free, use all sweet brown rice (1½ cups) and no wheat berries.

¾ cup soft wheat berries

¾ cup sweet brown rice

3 cups vegetable stock

1 thumb-size piece kombu

6 small sweet pumpkins

1 8-ounce package tempeh

2 tablespoons grapeseed oil

2 tablespoons balsamic vinegar

2 tablespoons mirin

½ teaspoon cumin seeds

½ teaspoon coriander seeds

¼ teaspoon celery seeds

3 leeks, sliced

2 garlic cloves, minced

8 ounces cremini mushrooms

2 teaspoons fresh oregano or thyme leaves

1 tablespoon prepared mustard

1 tablespoon tamari

1 cup chopped roasted cashews

Sea salt and freshly ground black pepper

PREPARING GRAINS

Soak wheat berries and rice for 1 hour in bowl with enough water to cover. Drain, rinse and place in pot with vegetable stock and kombu. Bring to boil, reduce heat, cover and simmer 25 minutes or until liquid is absorbed. Remove from heat and discard kombu.

ROASTING PUMPKINS

Preheat oven to 400°F. Cut off tops of pumpkins and remove seeds. Replace tops, arrange on cookie sheet and roast 30 minutes or until just tender. Remove from the oven and set aside.

PREPARING STUFFING

While pumpkins are roasting, cut tempeh into 4 pieces and steam 10 minutes. Remove from heat and set aside to cool. Crumble tempeh into medium skillet and sauté over medium heat in 1 tablespoon oil until lightly browned. Stir in vinegar and mirin. Remove from heat and add mixture to grains.

Heat remaining tablespoon of oil in skillet over medium heat. Add cumin, coriander and celery seeds and stir. Add leeks, garlic, mushrooms and oregano and sauté 5 minutes. Deglaze as needed with 1 tablespoon of water at a time. Add to grains.

In small bowl, whisk together mustard and 1 tablespoon tamari. Season with salt and pepper and add to grains along with roasted cashews.

ASSEMBLING

Toss grain mixture to combine all ingredients, stuff into pumpkins and cover with tops. Place on cookie sheet, roast 40–45 minutes until pumkins are cooked through and serve.

SERVES 6

Roasted Kabocha Squash and Creminis with Fresh Herbs

KABOCHA SQUASH HAS A SWEET AND THICK FLESH that requires very little fuss and cooks up surprisingly tender and delicious. When selecting kabocha, look for ones with smooth dark green outer skins. Irregularities on the skin are tough spots and should be cut away.

---

2   small or 1 large
    kabocha squash

2   leeks, sliced lengthwise
    and cut into ½-inch strips

3   tablespoons balsamic
    vinegar

3   tablespoons extra
    virgin olive oil

1   teaspoon coarse sea salt

1   pound cremini
    mushrooms, wiped clean

1   tablespoon minced
    fresh rosemary

1   tablespoon minced
    fresh sage

Preheat oven to 425°F.

Wash squash well, cut in half and remove seeds. Chop into bite-size pieces (leaving skin on) and toss in large bowl with leeks. Add vinegar, oil and salt. Spread onto cookie sheet and roast 10 minutes. Remove from oven, add mushrooms and continue roasting another 10 minutes. Sprinkle with rosemary and sage and roast a final 10 minutes (a total of 30 minutes). Remove from oven and serve.

SERVES 6

Kabocha Squash Stuffed with Brown Rice and Chickpea Pilaf

HEARTY KABOCHA MAKES A GREAT EDIBLE SERVING DISH for a variety of stuffings, including sweet brown rice, wild rice and quinoa.

---

1   kabocha squash

Extra virgin olive oil

½   cup chopped toasted pecans

BROWN RICE STUFFING

1   cup medium grain brown rice

2   cups water

1   thumb-size piece kombu

⅓   cup currants

1   teaspoon ground allspice

1   tablespoon dried dill

2   tablespoons grapeseed oil

1   onion, chopped

1½   cups cooked chickpeas

½   cup toasted pine nuts

¼   cup chopped fresh parsley

Juice of 1 lemon

Sea salt and freshly ground black pepper

Soak rice for 1 hour in bowl with enough water to cover. Drain, place rice in pot with 2 cups fresh water, kombu, currants, allspice and dill. Bring to boil, then reduce heat, cover and simmer 30 minutes or until water is absorbed. Set aside to cool.

ROASTING SQUASH

Preheat oven to 400°F. Wash squash well and cut in half from top to bottom. Remove seeds and rub skin and flesh with oil. Place cut side down on cookie sheet and roast 25 minutes or until soft (time will vary according to size of squash).

PREPARING STUFFING

In large skillet over medium heat, sauté onion in grapeseed oil until soft (about 3 minutes). Remove kombu from rice and discard. Add rice and chickpeas to onion and sauté 3 minutes. Remove from heat and toss with pine nuts, parsley and lemon juice. Season to taste with salt and pepper.

FINISHING

Slice cooked squash into boats, place on individual plates or group on a platter. Spoon brown rice stuffing over the center so that it spills down on each side, sprinkle with toasted pecans and serve.

SERVES 4

Silky Sweet Potato Pie

CHICKPEA FLOUR IS RICH AND CREAMY and imparts wonderful texture and taste when used in baking. Combined with pecans, this crust becomes much more than a simple shell for a delicious filling. I serve this savory and sweet pie as a side dish but have also been known to sneak a piece for breakfast!

CRUST
1½ cups pecans
¼   cup chickpea flour
2   tablespoons canola oil
2   tablespoons maple syrup
Pinch of sea salt

FILLING
3   medium sweet potatoes
¼   cup maple syrup
¼   cup rice milk
1   tablespoon vanilla extract
¼   teaspoon sea salt
½   teaspoon cinnamon
¼   teaspoon nutmeg
1   tablespoon arrowroot
1   teaspoon agar powder

Preheat oven to 350°F. Wash sweet potatoes, place on cookie sheet and bake until soft (time will vary according to size of potatoes). Remove from oven and set aside.

PREPARING CRUST
Meanwhile, chop pecans in food processor until they resemble fine meal. Add chickpea flour and process briefly to combine. Add oil, syrup and salt and process to form dough. Lightly grease a 9-inch pie plate with canola oil, add dough and press to form even crust (about ¼-inch thick). Pierce several times with a fork and bake 12 minutes. Remove from oven and set on wire rack to cool.

PREPARING FILLING
When sweet potatoes are cool enough to handle, remove skins and cut into large pieces. Place in cleaned food processor bowl, and add maple syrup, rice milk, vanilla, salt, cinnamon, nutmeg, arrowroot and agar powder. Process until smooth.

FINISHING
Pour filling into cooled pie crust, cover pie edges with foil and bake 50 minutes to 1 hour until lightly browned. Remove from oven and cool completely on wire rack. Serve at room temperature or cold.

SERVES 6–8

Refried Pinto Beans with Chiles

LEGUMES DON'T GET EASIER THAN THIS! Pinto beans are creamy and savory and require little fuss. I enjoy these beans as a side dish, stuffed into tacos and burritos, or served simply with brown rice, chopped tomato, lettuce and avocado.

3	garlic cloves, minced
1	small onion, diced
2	tablespoons grapeseed oil
4	cups cooked pinto beans
2	4-ounce cans chopped green chiles
1	teaspoon chile powder
1	teaspoon ground cumin
½	teaspoon sea salt
2	tablespoons lime juice
Chopped fresh cilantro for garnish	

In sauté pan or Dutch oven over medium heat, sauté garlic and onion in oil until soft (about 3 minutes). Add beans and remaining ingredients except cilantro and sauté another 3–4 minutes. With the back of a wooden spoon, gently mash the beans to your desired consistency. I like my finished product to be fairly chunky so I mash only half the ingredients. Remove from heat, top with cilantro and serve.

SERVES 6

Millet, Aduki Beans and Corn with Lemon Dressing

THIS RECIPE COMBINES SAVORY, NUTTY MILLET with sweet corn and sour lemon for a dish that is as pleasing to the eye as it is to the palate. For a complete meal, serve this dish warm with greens or enjoy it chilled for a light lunch or snack.

---

1   cup millet

2   cups water

Pinch of sea salt

2   cups cooked aduki beans, rinsed well

¼   cup diced red onion

1   cup corn, fresh or frozen and thawed

½   cup chopped fresh parsley

DRESSING

2   tablespoons extra virgin olive oil

2   tablespoons lemon juice

¼   teaspoon ground cumin

Zest of 1 lemon

Sea salt and freshly ground black pepper

Place millet, water and pinch of salt in rice cooker or large pot over high heat. Cover and bring to boil. Reduce heat to low and cook covered until all water is absorbed (about 25 minutes). Remove from heat and let cool 5 minutes (so that it does not turn to mush when fluffed).

Fluff millet and add aduki beans, onion, corn and parsley. In small bowl, whisk together dressing ingredients and pour over grain mixture. Fold to combine and serve. If serving chilled, fluff again gently with fork before serving.

SERVES 6

White Beans and Escarole

I FIRST TASTED ESCAROLE WITH WHITE BEANS when my mother-in-law made it. I remember the aroma of the sautéed garlic luring me into her kitchen and the escarole melting in my mouth. From the very first bite, I was hooked. She makes hers with a bit of stock and *ancini di pepe* (tiny pasta pearls). I like to serve mine with a crusty sourdough or Italian bread, which comes in handy for cleaning the plate when you're done!

---

6   garlic cloves, minced

2   tablespoons extra virgin olive oil

3½ cups cooked great northern or navy beans

2   large heads escarole, chopped

2   tablespoons flax seed oil

5   dashes ume plum vinegar

Gomasio

In Dutch oven over medium heat, sauté garlic in olive oil until soft (about 2 minutes). Add beans and escarole and stir until escarole starts to wilt. Continue cooking 3 minutes. Remove from heat, drizzle with flax oil and vinegar and toss to combine. Sprinkle with gomasio and serve.

VARIATION

To turn this dish into a rich, nondairy cream soup, add 3–4 cups vegetable stock, simmer 5 minutes, purée with handheld blender and serve.

SERVES 4 as a side dish

Scrambled Tofu

THIS DISH MAKES A QUICK AND EASY PROTEIN-FILLED BREAKFAST.
For a colorful and complete meal, try it served with salsa and sautéed greens or wrap it all up in a corn tortilla for a meal on the go.

---

1   pound fresh firm or extra firm tofu

2   tablespoons extra virgin olive oil

1   onion, chopped

1   carrot, grated

1   cup cremini mushrooms, thinly sliced

1   tablespoon tamari

Wrap tofu in towels and press to remove excess water.

In large skillet over medium heat, sauté onion in olive oil until soft (about 3 minutes). Add carrot and mushrooms and sauté 3 minutes longer until mushrooms are soft. Mash tofu and add to the pan. Season with tamari and sauté 5 minutes. Remove from heat and serve.

SERVES 4

Marinated Tofu with Ginger Cashew Dipping Sauce

I LOVE TO KEEP BAKED TOFU IN THE HOUSE as a snack, but this rich and delicious dipping sauce makes it great for mealtime as well. Be sure to cook enough to compensate for the pieces that you'll sneak before it gets to the table! Serve on skewers for a fun presentation.

---

2   pounds firm tofu (not silken)

1   tablespoon grated fresh ginger

¼   cup Bragg Liquid Aminos

1   tablespoon chickpea or mellow white miso

1   garlic clove, minced

1   tablespoon toasted sesame oil

⅓   cup orange juice

DIPPING SAUCE

1   tablespoon grapeseed oil

2   garlic cloves, minced

1   tablespoon grated fresh ginger

2   scallions, minced

3   tablespoons tamari

2   tablespoons maple syrup

⅓   cup coconut milk

1   cup finely ground cashews

1   tablespoon toasted sesame oil

Hot pepper sauce

PREPARING TOFU

Slice tofu lengthwise into ½-inch strips. In shallow baking dish, combine ginger, liquid aminos, miso, garlic, sesame oil, juice and 2 tablespoons water. Place tofu in dish and coat with marinade (flipping to coat both sides). Set aside to marinate 30 minutes.

Preheat oven to 400°F. Place tofu on ungreased baking sheet and save leftover marinade. Bake 15 minutes. Remove pan from oven, flip tofu, baste with remaining marinade and bake another 15 minutes.

PREPARING SAUCE

In small skillet over medium heat, gently sauté garlic and ginger in grapeseed oil for 2 minutes. Add scallions and sauté another 2 minutes. Add tamari, syrup, coconut milk, cashews and ¼ cup water and stir to combine. Increase heat briefly and then reduce heat and simmer 10 minutes, stirring occasionally, to combine flavors. Remove from heat and season to taste with toasted sesame oil and hot pepper sauce.

Serve tofu with sauce on side or drizzled on top.

SERVES 4

Tofu Kale Lasagna

THIS IS ONE OF MY MOST REQUESTED RECIPES, and not just because it's my daughter's favorite. Tofu can be used to achieve many different tastes and textures in lasagna. I've used fresh firm tofu in this version, but you can substitute silken tofu for a cheesier texture or freeze your tofu first for a meatier texture.

5–7	sun-dried tomatoes
12	lasagna noodles
4	garlic cloves, minced
1	large onion, chopped
6	tablespoons extra virgin olive oil
8–10	ounces cremini mushrooms, sliced
2	pounds fresh firm tofu
2	tablespoons mirin
2	teaspoons dried basil
2	teaspoons dried parsley
2	bunches kale, finely chopped
	Sea salt and freshly ground black pepper
5	cups tomato sauce
1½	cups grated soy or rice mozzarella

Preheat oven to 375°F. In small bowl, soak sun-dried tomatoes in enough hot water to cover. When soft, drain, chop and set aside. Cook lasagna noodles until just soft. Drain and set aside.

PREPARING FILLING

In large pot over medium heat, sauté garlic and onions until soft. Add mushrooms and sauté 3 minutes. Drain tofu, wrap in towels, press to remove excess water and crumble into pot. Add mirin, sun-dried tomatoes, basil and parsley and sauté 5 minutes. Fold in kale, cover and cook 3 minutes. Season to taste with salt and pepper and remove from heat.

ASSEMBLING

Spread ½ cup tomato sauce over bottom of 9 x 12-inch lasagna pan. Place single layer of noodles over sauce and cover with half the kale mixture. Cover with 1½ cups tomato sauce. Sprinkle with ½ cup soy cheese. Cover with another layer of noodles and remaining kale and tofu. Add 1½ cups sauce, ½ cup soy mozzarella, and final layer of noodles, ½ cup sauce and remaining mozzarella. Cover tightly with foil and bake 35 minutes. Remove foil and bake 10 more minutes. Remove from oven and set aside for 10 minutes before serving.

VARIATION

For a meatier texture, freeze tofu first, then defrost, press out excess liquid, place in food processor and process to crumble. Add to filling as described above. Add extra liquid before adding kale – I use ½ cup tomato sauce thinned with ½ cup water. Add an additional cup of sauce to the tofu mixture to season. Add kale and proceed as above.

SERVES 8

Baked Maple Mustard Tempeh

STEAMED TEMPEH PUFFS UP, allowing it to absorb more flavors and making it a nice complement to dark leafy greens. If I can keep myself from eating the tempeh straight out of the oven, I like to serve this dish with whole grains and vegetables or stuffed in a sandwich with watercress, grated carrots and avocado.

2	8-ounce packages tempeh
¼	cup extra virgin olive oil
2	garlic cloves, minced
2	tablespoons prepared mustard
2	tablespoons maple syrup or molasses
2	tablespoons lime juice
2	tablespoons tamari

Slice tempeh across into ½-inch strips and steam 10 minutes.

In shallow baking dish, whisk together oil, garlic, mustard, maple syrup, lime juice and tamari. Place steamed tempeh in marinade and flip to coat each side. Marinate for 30 minutes.

Preheat oven to 425°F.

Place tempeh with marinade in oven and roast 10 minutes. Remove from oven, flip tempeh and return to roast another 10 minutes. Remove from oven, serve hot or refrigerate for later use.

SERVES 4

Seitan Walnut Stuffed Collard Greens

AFTER THE FIRST FROST, collard greens in New England get heartier and sweeter. This dish is great for company because you can make it in advance, cover it with foil, refrigerate and then bake it just before your guests arrive. Ginger Pear Sauce *(page 147)* is a perfect accompaniment.

8	large collard green leaves
½	cup plus 2 tablespoons grated mochi

FILLING
1	pound seitan
1	tablespoon grapeseed oil
1	small onion, chopped
8–10	cremini mushrooms, diced
½	cup dried cranberries
¼	cup mirin
1	cup toasted and chopped walnuts
1	tablespoon dried sage

Sea salt and freshly ground black pepper

SAUCE
1	cup vegetable stock
1	cup water

Juice of 1 lemon
¼	cup brown rice syrup

Bring medium pot of water to boil. Cut stems at base of collard leaf and discard. Submerge whole leaves in boiling water for 1 minute. Drain, rinse with cold water and set aside.

PREPARING FILLING
Grind seitan in food processor using the pulse setting. In large pan over medium heat, sauté onion in oil until soft. Add mushrooms and cook 3 minutes. Add seitan, cranberries, mirin and walnuts and cook to heat through. Add sage, and salt and pepper to taste and remove from heat.

PREPARING SAUCE
In medium pot, combine stock, water, lemon juice and rice syrup. Place over medium heat and cook for 4 minutes or until syrup dissolves.

ASSEMBLING
Preheat oven to 350°F.

Lay one collard leaf flat on cutting board. On the largest part of the leaf, sprinkle 1 tablespoon of grated mochi plus enough filling to cover a third of the wide end of the leaf. Fold sides of leaf over filling, then roll the whole thing toward the stem and place it, stem side down, in baking dish. Repeat to fill the casserole and use all filling. Sprinkle top with remaining 2 tablespoons of mochi, pour sauce into dish, cover with foil and bake 30 minutes. Remove from oven and serve.

SERVES 6

Skillet Cornbread

CORNBREAD IS A MUST WITH EVERYTHING from Savory "Unbaked" Beans *(page 230)* to Sweet Potato and Black Bean Burritos *(page 268)*. The addition of whole corn kernels, red pepper and jalapeño pepper make this cornbread burst with flavor and color. For a richer taste, add one cup of shredded cheddar-style rice or soy cheese. I bake it the traditional southern way, in a seasoned cast-iron skillet, to produce a crisp outside. Serve it straight from the skillet for an authentic and easy presentation.

½   cup corn flour

½   cup yellow cornmeal

1   cup unbleached all-purpose flour

2   teaspoons powdered egg replacer

1   teaspoon baking powder

½   teaspoon baking soda

½   teaspoon salt

1   cup rice milk

3   tablespoons maple syrup

3   tablespoons extra virgin olive oil plus more for skillet

1   jalapeño, seeded and minced

½   red bell pepper, minced

1   cup corn, fresh or frozen

Preheat oven to 375°F.

In large bowl, combine all dry ingredients. In separate bowl, combine all wet ingredients including the jalapeño, red pepper and corn. Pour wet ingredients into dry and mix to combine.

Heat a well-seasoned 10-inch cast-iron skillet over medium-high heat until hot. Pour in enough olive oil to coat the bottom and sides. Pour batter into skillet and spread it out evenly. Remove from burner, place in oven and bake 20 minutes or until a toothpick inserted in center comes out clean. Remove from oven and place on wire rack to cool and set before serving.

SERVES 8

Multigrain Pilaf with Toasted Sunflower Seeds

SUNFLOWER SEEDS IN THIS RECIPE BRING OUT the nutty flavors of the grains and turn an otherwise ordinary dish into something special. Experiment with different grain and seed combinations for a variety of tastes and textures.

⅔ cup sunflower seeds

½ cup millet

½ cup hulled barley (not pearl)

½ cup sweet brown rice

3 cups water

1 thumb-size piece kombu

1 large onion, diced

1 tablespoon extra virgin olive oil

Soak barley and sweet brown rice for 1 hour in bowl with enough water to cover. Drain, rinse and drain again.

Meanwhile, preheat oven to 250°F.

Spread sunflower seeds on cookie sheet and roast 8–10 minutes until golden brown. Remove from oven and set aside to cool.

Rinse millet, place in large Dutch oven over medium heat and dry-roast until fragrant. Add barley, sweet brown rice, 3 cups water and kombu and bring to boil. Cover, reduce heat and simmer until water is absorbed (about 35 minutes). Remove from heat, discard kombu and let set 5 minutes before fluffing.

In large skillet over medium heat, sauté onion in olive oil until soft. Add to grains and stir to combine. Top with sunflower seeds and serve.

SERVES 8

Pan-Roasted Millet
with Pumpkin Seeds

THE FIRST TIME I MADE MILLET FOR MY CHILDREN it was not a hit. The next time I made it I used four times the amount of water and called it porridge. They devoured it. After a year of porridge, I made the millet with the regular amount of water and served it with dinner. They didn't even flinch. Both said, "Yeah, porridge!" and continued to eat it as if I hadn't changed a thing.

---

1   cup millet
1   cup water
1   cup vegetable stock
    Pinch of sea salt
2   tablespoons flax seed oil
½   teaspoon ume
    plum vinegar
¼   cup plain or tamari-
    roasted pumpkin seeds

Rinse and drain millet. Place in Dutch oven over medium heat and dry-roast until water is absorbed and millet starts to give off a nutty aroma. Add water, stock and salt, cover, reduce heat and simmer until all liquid is absorbed (about 25 minutes). Set aside to cool slightly then fluff with fork, drizzle with flax seed oil and vinegar and toss. Top with toasted pumpkin seeds and serve.

SERVES 4

Quinoa with Almonds and Currants

QUINOA IS MUCH LIGHTER THAN OTHER GRAINS and every bit as satisfying. Cooking quinoa with currants as I do here imparts a sweetness that is then balanced with savory and pungent spices. Serve it as a side dish, or press the quinoa into small ramekins, then release the molded quinoa onto plates composed for individual servings.

1½ cups quinoa

2¼ cups water

¼ cup currants

Pinch of sea salt

1 tablespoon extra virgin olive oil

1 red onion, diced

¼ teaspoon ground cinnamon

¼ teaspoon ground ginger

¼ teaspoon ground coriander

⅛ teaspoon ground turmeric

¾ teaspoon ground cumin

3 tablespoons toasted sliced almonds

¼ cup chopped fresh parsley

Sea salt and freshly ground black pepper

Rinse quinoa and place in large pot or rice cooker with water, currants and salt. Bring to boil, then reduce heat and simmer 15 minutes or until all water is absorbed. Let cool slightly before fluffing with fork.

In large skillet over medium heat, sauté onion and spices in oil until soft (about 5 minutes). Fold into cooked quinoa along with almonds and parsley. Season to taste with salt and pepper and serve.

Note: To make this dish less sweet, cook quinoa without currants and add them at the end with the almonds and parsley.

SERVES 6

Stovetop Barley with Sweet Vegetables

THIS IS THE QUINTESSENTIAL "MEAL IN A POT." When I first taught this recipe in one of my classes, I purposely neglected to mention that Brussels sprouts were a significant ingredient. Once there, all felt obliged to at least try a taste, and every Brussels sprout hater loved this dish!

1	cup hulled barley (not pearl)
½	cup brown rice
1	thumb-size piece kombu
2	tablespoons tamari
4½–5	cups water or vegetable stock
1	onion, chopped
3	carrots, chopped
1	rutabaga, peeled and cubed
12	Brussels sprouts, halved
1	small fennel bulb, halved, cored and sliced

Extra virgin olive oil

Ume plum vinegar

Chopped fresh parsley for garnish

Soak barley and brown rice together for 1 hour in bowl with enough water to cover. Rinse and drain grains and place in large pot or Dutch oven. Add kombu, tamari and water or stock. Cover and bring to boil.

When grains start to boil, add vegetables in order listed. Cover, reduce heat and simmer 2–2½ hours. Remove from heat and drizzle with olive oil and several dashes of vinegar. Garnish with parsley and serve directly from the pot.

SERVES 6

Sweet Dumpling Squash with Orange-Scented Quinoa Stuffing

DUMPLING SQUASH IS NOT ONLY SWEET AND DELICIOUS, it also makes a very pretty presentation. Serve it sliced into boat shapes, cut into rings or stuffed with grains, as I've done here.

6	small dumpling squash (one per person)
2	tablespoons extra virgin olive oil plus more for rubbing squash
2	cups quinoa
3½	cups water
	Pinch of sea salt
6	shallots, diced
1	pound cremini mushrooms, thinly sliced
2	tablespoons mirin
3	stalks celery, diced
1	cup dried cranberries
½	teaspoon ground nutmeg
1	cup toasted pine nuts
2	tablespoons walnut oil
2	tablespoons fresh orange peel
½	cup chopped fresh parsley
	Sea salt and freshly ground black pepper

ROASTING SQUASH

Preheat oven to 450°F. Wash squash well. Rub each squash with oil and place whole on parchment-lined cookie sheet. Bake 45 minutes or until just soft (time will vary depending on size of squash). Remove from oven and set aside.

PREPARING QUINOA

Rinse and drain quinoa. Place in large pot with water and salt and bring to boil. Cover, reduce heat and simmer 15 minutes or until all liquid is absorbed. Set aside to cool slightly.

PREPARING STUFFING

In large skillet over medium heat, sauté shallots and mushrooms in oil until soft. Add mirin, celery, cranberries and nutmeg and sauté 3 minutes longer. Fluff quinoa with fork and add to the skillet. Remove from heat, fold in pine nuts, walnut oil, orange peel and parsley. Season to taste with salt and pepper.

ASSEMBLING

Carefully cut a circle around the stem of each squash to remove the "lid." Scoop out seeds and fill with stuffing. Top with a sprinkle of fresh parsley, set lid on side and serve.

SERVES 6

Wild Rice, Barley and Arame Salad

THIS SALAD COMBINES SOOTHING BARLEY (particularly healing to the stomach), with wild rice (high in protein) and arame (a sea vegetable high in absorbable calcium, iron and minerals). Talk about a powerhouse of a meal! Serve this salad as a side dish or enjoy its hearty flavors and textures as an energizing snack, a stand-alone salad or a light dinner.

½ cup hulled barley (not pearl)

1 cup wild rice

3½ cups water

Pinch of sea salt

1 cup dried arame

¾ cup roasted cashews, coarsely chopped

4 scallions, chopped

¼ cup diced roasted red pepper

¼ cup toasted sesame seeds

3 tablespoons toasted sesame oil

1 tablespoon tamari

1½ teaspoons apple cider vinegar

Soak barley for 1 hour in bowl with enough water to cover. Drain, rinse and place in rice cooker or large pot. Add wild rice, water and salt. Cook 40 minutes or until liquid is absorbed. Set aside to cool before fluffing.

Meanwhile soak arame for 10 minutes in bowl with enough hot water to cover. Drain, rinse and set aside.

In large bowl, combine cooked grains, cashews, scallions, roasted pepper, arame and sesame seeds. In small bowl, whisk together sesame oil, tamari and vinegar. Pour over grains and toss to evenly coat. Serve at room temperature.

Note: If you make this salad in advance, add cashews and scallions just before serving so they don't get soggy. Store salad in airtight container in refrigerator for up to 4 days.

SERVES 6

Apple Crisp

A GUILT-FREE VERSION OF AN ALL-TIME FAVORITE! To make the topping gluten-free, use brown rice flour instead of whole wheat and substitute chopped nuts for the oats.

FILLING

12 apples (peeled, unpeeled or both), cored and sliced

¼ cup maple syrup

2 teaspoons ground cinnamon

⅓ cup dried currants

1 tablespoon whole wheat pastry flour or brown rice flour

TOPPING

2 cups rolled oats

1 cup whole wheat flour or brown rice flour

½ cup chopped walnuts

1 tablespoon ground cinnamon

½ cup maple syrup

½ cup canola oil

Preheat oven to 375°F.

To prepare filling, place apples in large bowl. Fold in syrup, cinnamon and currants. Sprinkle on flour and gently fold until combined. Spread mixture into 9 x 12-inch baking casserole.

To make topping, use the same mixing bowl and combine oats, flour, nuts and cinnamon. In separate bowl, whisk together syrup and oil, add to dry ingredients and mix until crumbly. Spread topping evenly over apples, cover with foil and bake 30 minutes. Remove foil and bake an additional 20 minutes or until apples are cooked through. Remove from oven and serve.

SERVES 8–10

Ginger Pear Crisp

CRISPS ARE SO EASY TO MAKE, and in my family they're served not only for dessert but for breakfast or a midday snack, too. This one tastes great with a scoop of vanilla bean ice (or rice) cream. As with my Apple Crisp recipe *(page 189)*, this is easily made gluten-free by substituting brown rice flour for wheat and using chopped nuts in place of oats for the topping.

FILLING

8	large pears (Bosc or D'Anjou work well)
¼	cup maple syrup
1	teaspoon almond extract
2	teaspoons grated fresh ginger

Zest of 1 orange

½	cup apple juice or cider
1	tablespoon arrowroot

TOPPING

2	cups rolled oats
1	cup whole wheat pastry flour
1	cup toasted sliced almonds

Pinch of sea salt

½	cup maple syrup
⅓	cup canola oil
1	teaspoon almond extract

Preheat oven to 350°F.

Peel, core and slice pears and place in large casserole.

In medium bowl, combine syrup, almond extract, ginger, orange zest and apple juice. Whisk in arrowroot until dissolved, pour mixture evenly over pears and set aside.

Prepare topping in separate bowl by combining oats, flour, almonds and sea salt. In separate bowl, whisk together syrup, oil and almond extract. Add wet ingredients to dry, fold to combine, then sprinkle over pears. Cover with foil and bake 35 minutes. Remove foil and bake another 15 minutes or until crumb topping is crisp and lightly browned. Remove from oven and serve warm.

SERVES 8–10

Maple Poached Pears

POACHED PEARS ARE SIMPLE AND SATISFYING and will fill your house with the most wonderful aroma. Serve them on their own, with ice cream or in a small pool of syrup and topped with chopped nuts. Save the syrup to serve over ice cream, pancakes or French toast or mixed with hot tea for a special warming after-dinner drink.

4–6   ripe, but firm, pears
1   cup water
1   cup maple syrup

Choose any or all of
the following options:
Zest of 1 lemon or orange
1   teaspoon vanilla extract
4–5   whole cloves
1   cinnamon stick
1   1-inch piece gingerroot,
        peeled and thinly sliced

In large pot over medium heat, combine water, syrup, zest and choice of flavorings and bring to simmer. Cut pears in half, remove cores and place in simmering syrup. Cook 20 minutes then remove from heat, let cool slightly and serve.

SERVES 4

Green Tea Poached Pears with Pomegranate Glaze and Pistachios

THIS DESSERT HAS A LITTLE SOMETHING FOR EVERYONE. Cool and refreshing pears, bitter green tea, salty pistachios and plenty of color for a beautiful presentation.

---

6   pears, peeled, halved and cored

3   green tea teabags

6   cups water

½   cup maple syrup

½   cup roasted pistachios, finely chopped

Mint leaves for garnish

GLAZE

1½ cups pomegranate juice

1   cup water

½   cup maple syrup

1½ tablespoons arrowroot dissolved in 3 tablespoons water

In large pot, bring water to boil. Add teabags and maple syrup, turn off heat, cover and steep 5 minutes (longer steeping will make tea bitter). Remove teabags, add pears and bring to simmer. Poach pears until tender but still held together (6–10 minutes depending on ripeness). Remove poached pears with slotted spoon and let cool.

Make glaze in medium pot by stirring juice, water and syrup together over medium-high heat until liquid is reduced by half. Remove from heat and immediately stir in dissolved arrowroot. Refrigerate until ready to use.

To serve, place pear halves decoratively on each plate, drizzle with pomegranate glaze and top with chopped pistachios. Garnish with mint leaves and serve.

SERVES 6

Tofu Pumpkin Pie with Gingersnap Crust

EVERY THANKSGIVING I MAKE TWO OF THESE PIES—one for the company and one to enjoy with our leftovers. An easy way to make a terrific crust is with store-bought gingersnaps. If possible, make this pie a day ahead to allow pie to set and flavors to blend.

CRUST

2   heaping cups gingersnaps
¼   cup canola oil
¼   cup maple syrup

FILLING

12   ounces silken extra firm or firm tofu
2   cups cooked pumpkin pureé
½   cup maple syrup
1   teaspoon vanilla extract
1   generous tablespoon pumpkin pie spice

Preheat oven to 350°F.

Crumble gingersnaps, either in food processor, or by placing them in a plastic bag and crushing them with a rolling pin. Place crumbs in bowl, add oil and syrup and stir until mixture sticks together. Add to lightly greased 9-inch pie plate and press to form ¼-inch thick crust.

Wrap tofu in towels and press to remove excess water. In clean food processor bowl, process tofu until smooth. Scrape down sides of bowl and process again to incorporate all the tofu. Add all remaining filling ingredients and process until smooth and well combined. Pour into pie crust, cover edges with foil to prevent burning and bake 50 minutes or until lightly browned. Remove from oven, cool and serve.

SERVES 8

Glazed Oranges with Pomegranate Seeds

POMEGRANATES ARE IN SEASON for such a short time that I like to use them as much as possible to satisfy me until the next year. This is a very simple yet decadent, refreshing and festive-looking dessert.

---

4   oranges
1   pomegranate
½   cup water
¼   cup maple syrup
1   cinnamon stick
5   cloves
Zest of 1 orange
Zest and juice of 1 lemon

Remove peel and outside skin from oranges and slice across into rounds. Place in serving dish and set aside. Cut pomegranate in half. Remove seeds from one half and add to bowl with oranges. Set the other half aside.

In small pot over medium heat, combine water with syrup, cinnamon stick, cloves, zests and lemon juice. Bring to boil, reduce heat and simmer 7 minutes to reduce to a glaze. Remove from heat. Squeeze remaining pomegranate through a sieve to get juice and stir into glaze. Pour over oranges and serve warm or chilled.

SERVES 4

Chocolate Lover's Tart

LET'S FACE IT – WE ALL HAVE CRAVINGS we simply can't deny! You
might as well make peace with them and enjoy. This recipe comes together
so easily, you may find yourself making it far too often. But, seeing as it
doesn't call for eggs, brown sugar, butter or even white flour, you can go
ahead and enjoy it without nearly as much guilt.

CRUST

2 cups pecans
1 cup brown rice flour
¼ cup cocoa powder
¼ teaspoon sea salt
⅓ cup canola oil
⅓ cup maple syrup

FILLING

12½ ounces firm silken tofu
½ cup cashew butter
¼ cup maple syrup
1 teaspoon vanilla extract
Pinch of sea salt
1 cup semisweet dark chocolate chips
1 6-ounce block dark chocolate for shaving (I like 70%)

Preheat oven to 350°F. Lightly oil an 11-inch tart pan.

PREPARING CRUST

Combine pecans, rice flour, cocoa and salt in food processor to make a
crumb-like mixture. Add oil and syrup and process to form a moist ball.
Place ball in tart pan and press to form crust. Pierce several times with
a fork and bake 15 minutes or until lightly browned. Remove from oven
and set on wire rack to cool completely.

MAKING FILLING

Whip tofu in food processor until smooth. Add cashew butter, syrup,
vanilla and salt and process until well combined. In small pan over low
heat, melt chocolate chips, then add to food processor and blend until
combined.

FINISHING

Pour chocolate mixture into tart shell, smooth top with spatula and
refrigerate at least 30 minutes. With a sturdy chef's knife, shave
chocolate from block, spread evenly over tart and serve.

SERVES 8–10

Winter is the time of promise because there is so little to do – or because you can now and then permit yourself the luxury of thinking so.

STANLEY CRAWFORD

Winter

The early weeks of winter feel like one long celebration of food as I taste my way through a never-ending series of holiday parties. Aromatic roasted nuts, sugary winter squashes, savory wild rices, exotic mushrooms and decadent sweets tempt me at every turn and prove that all food tastes best when shared with friends and family. By mid-January, I am completely content with winter's simple menu of warming soups and stews, casseroles, roasted roots and sautéed greens. Soups and sauces simmer all day in my kitchen and fill my home with wonderful aromas. The freezer and pantry overflow with freshly frozen and canned foods — the summer's pesto, berries from the picking patch and freshly pickled beets and beans — all ready to add just enough spice to winter's comforting menu. Everything about winter, from its short, cold days to its simple and sweet tastes, allows my mind and body to rest.

WINTER

Maple Apple Vinaigrette

I LEARNED EARLY ON THAT MY CHILDREN will eat anything they get to make with the handheld blender. I let them make salad dressings all of the time. The result? They love when I serve salad and eat every last bite without fail. Some of their combinations are suspect, but this one is a winner!

1   garlic clove, minced

1   shallot, minced

1   tablespoon apple butter

2   tablespoons prepared mustard

2   tablespoons maple syrup

2   teaspoons dried dill

1   teaspoon dried parsley

1   tablespoon lemon juice or apple cider vinegar

1   tablespoon toasted sesame oil

¼   cup red wine vinegar

½   cup extra virgin olive oil

Sea salt and freshly ground black pepper

Place all ingredients in bowl and whisk together. A handheld blender will emulsify vinaigrette but is not necessary. Thin vinaigrette by adding water 1 tablespoon at a time until you reach the desired consistency. Store refrigerated for up to 1 week.

MAKES 1½ cups

Pomegranate Vinaigrette

THIS SIMPLE SALAD DRESSING takes people by surprise every time. Perhaps it is pomegranate's reputation as the fruit of the gods, or its rich supply of vitamin C, folic acid and antioxidants all packaged together in this sweet and exotic juice – whichever the case, this vinaigrette can turn even the most simple salad into something special.

1   garlic clove, minced

1   shallot, minced

⅓   cup pomegranate juice

½   cup extra virgin olive oil

2   tablespoons balsamic vinegar

1   tablespoon zesty honey mustard (I like Honeycup brand)

Sea salt

In medium bowl, whisk together all ingredients by hand or with handheld blender. Season to taste with salt. Vinaigrette will keep refrigerated for 1 week.

MAKES 1 cup

Mexican Layer Dip

I REMEMBER WHEN MY MOTHER MADE THIS DIP for parties when I was a child. When we eliminated dairy from our diets, this dip, sadly, went by the wayside. Years later, after discovering the wonders of tofu, my mother reintroduced this nondairy version and it exceeded my memories and expectations.

---

16 ounces prepared
    bean dip of choice

2   4-ounce cans chopped
    green chiles

4   avocados

2   tablespoons lime juice

1   teaspoon sea salt

¼   teaspoon garlic powder

2   cups shredded soy
    or rice cheese

2   cups sliced scallions

2   cups chopped tomatoes

1½ cups pitted and chopped
    black olives

Tortilla chips

TOFU SOUR CREAM

16 ounces silken extra
    firm tofu

1   tablespoon canola oil

2   tablespoons lemon juice

1   teaspoon brown
    rice vinegar

Pinch of sea salt

1   tablespoon taco seasoning

PREPARING SOUR CREAM

In food processor, combine tofu, oil, lemon juice, brown rice vinegar and salt. Process until smooth. Add taco seasoning and pulse to combine.

ASSEMBLING

Spread bean dip evenly over the bottom of a 10 x 15-inch casserole. Top with tofu sour cream. Spread chiles evenly over tofu sour cream. Slice avocados in half, remove pits, scoop out flesh and place in large bowl. Add lime juice, salt and garlic powder, mash to combine and spread on chiles. Sprinkle with soy or rice cheese, scallions, tomatoes and olives. Refrigerate and serve chilled with a basket of tortilla chips.

Olive Tapenade

I OFTEN PREPARE THIS TAPENADE FOR COMPANY and serve it with Garlic Crostini *(page 204)* as an appetizer or as an accompaniment to a pasta dinner. But I enjoy it even more the next day spread on toasted sourdough bread in a roasted vegetable or portobello mushroom sandwich.

---

2   garlic cloves, peeled

1½ cups kalamata olives, pitted

1   cup oil-cured black Greek olives, pitted

2   generous tablespoons capers

¼   teaspoon dried thyme

¼   cup fresh parsley

1   tablespoon lemon juice (plus more if desired)

Freshly ground black pepper

Extra virgin olive oil (as needed)

With food processor running, drop in garlic and mince. Turn processor off, add olives, capers, thyme, parsley, lemon juice and pepper to taste. Process until smooth, scraping down sides as needed. Add olive oil a little at a time to achieve the desired consistency. Adjust flavor with more lemon juice and transfer to bowl. Store in airtight container in refrigerator or freezer.

MAKES 1¼ cups

Garlic Crostini

I TEACH MY CHILDREN that white foods are generally filler foods and not nutritionally packed. Unfortunately, I don't always follow my own teaching. While the garlic and olive oil in this dish are heart-healthy, the real reason that I make crostini is that it's simply delicious whether served with mussels marinara, Olive Tapenade *(page 203)* or whatever your pleasure.

---

1 long, thin baguette

Extra virgin olive oil

2–3 garlic cloves, peeled

2–3 tablespoons dried herbs of choice (rosemary, thyme, basil or oregano)

Pinch of sea salt

Preheat oven to 450°F.

Cut baguette on the diagonal into thin slices and place side by side on cookie sheet. Brush top of each piece of bread with olive oil. Slice garlic cloves in half and rub them over each piece of bread. Place in oven and bake 3 minutes. Remove from oven, flip bread slices, brush the other side with oil and rub with garlic. Sprinkle with dried herbs and salt, return to oven and bake until lightly browned and crisp. Remove from oven and serve.

VARIATION

Brush bread slices with pesto, then toast as described above.

Note: Cut leftovers into cubes to use as croutons and freeze. When ready to use, place frozen cubes on a cookie sheet and bake at 350°F until crisp.

Cranberry Applesauce

EVERY FALL WE GO APPLE PICKING and return home with more apples than we can possibly consume. When we simply cannot eat any more apple crisp, I steam the rest to make applesauce. This simple version makes a sweet accompaniment to a savory winter meal. For a more traditional applesauce, use 1½ cups apple cider and a dash of cinnamon and omit the cranberry juice.

---

6   apples of choice,
    peeled and cored

1   cup water or apple cider

½   cup unsweetened
    cranberry juice

2   tablespoons maple syrup

Place apples in pot with water or cider and cranberry juice. Cover, bring to boil, reduce heat and simmer until apples are soft. Remove from heat, add syrup and purée with handheld blender. Serve warm or chilled. Store in airtight container in refrigerator or freezer.

SERVES 4

Golden Split Pea Soup

THIS BEAUTIFUL, GOLDEN, HIGH-PROTEIN SOUP gets better and better the longer it simmers on your stove. Serve it alone, over basmati rice or with a side of leafy greens for a satisfying and simple meal.

2	tablespoons extra virgin olive oil
1	large yellow onion, diced
4	garlic cloves, minced
4	stalks celery, diced
4	carrots, diced
2	cups chopped tomatoes
1	potato, peeled and diced
¼	cup mirin
2	tablespoons red wine vinegar
½	teaspoon powdered mustard
4	cups golden split peas
10	cups water
½	teaspoon sea salt
	Freshly ground black pepper
1	bay leaf

In large soup pot over medium heat, sauté onion and garlic in olive oil until soft. Add celery and carrots and sauté another 3 minutes. Add tomatoes, potato, mirin, vinegar and mustard and stir to combine. Rinse and drain split peas and add to pot along with remaining ingredients. Bring soup to boil, cover, reduce heat and simmer at least 4 hours, adding water as needed to thin. Remove bay leaf and serve.

Note: For a smoother texture, lightly purée soup with handheld blender before serving.

SERVES 8

Lentil Soup

THERE'S NOTHING LIKE A POT OF LENTIL SOUP that's been
simmering all day. If you have a hearty appetite, serve this over basmati
rice – a great combination – or add some steamed kale or collards for a
well-balanced and satisfying meal.

1	thumb-size piece kombu
2	tablespoons extra virgin olive oil
1	large onion, chopped
3	garlic cloves, minced
3	stalks celery, diced
3	carrots, diced
2	cups chopped tomatoes
¼	cup red wine
4	cups dried lentils
10	cups water or vegetable stock
1	tablespoon brown rice vinegar
2	tablespoons maple syrup
1	tablespoon molasses
1	tablespoon tamari
	Sea salt and freshly ground black pepper

Place kombu in bowl with enough water to cover and soak 10 minutes or until soft. Drain, mince and set aside. In large soup pot over medium heat, sauté onion and garlic in olive oil until soft (about 3 minutes). Add celery, carrots, tomatoes and red wine. Rinse lentils and add to pot along with water or stock. Add vinegar, syrup, molasses, tamari, kombu, and salt and pepper to taste. Stir, bring to boil, then reduce heat. Cover and simmer 2 hours. Adjust seasonings and serve.

VARIATION

For a richer, more decadent soup, add 2 tablespoons cocoa powder along with molasses.

SERVES 8

Goodness Soup

MY MOTHER COINED THE NAME FOR THIS SOUP when I was a child. We never knew what was in it – we just knew it would be thick and delicious. Now that I'm a parent, I appreciate this soup even more. Not only does it allow me to make soup out of whatever I have on hand, but it helps me hide a host of nutritious foods that are otherwise a challenge to get my children to eat. Use this recipe as a template and add or substitute freely with whatever vegetables happen to be in your refrigerator!

2	thumb-size pieces kombu
2	tablespoons extra virgin olive oil
1	onion, chopped
1	pound mushrooms (any variety), chopped
5	carrots, chopped
3	stalks celery, chopped
1½	cups cooked navy or great northern beans
1	cup hulled barley, rinsed
1	cup lentils, rinsed
1	tablespoon dried parsley
1	tablespoon dried basil
1	bay leaf
¼	cup mirin or white wine
2	tablespoons tamari
12	cups water
	Sea salt and freshly ground black pepper

Place kombu in bowl with enough water to cover, soak 10 minutes or until soft. Drain, mince and set aside.

In large pot over medium heat, sauté onion and mushrooms in olive oil for 5 minutes. Lower heat and add carrots, celery, beans, barley, lentils, parsley, basil, bay leaf, mirin and tamari. Stir to combine, add water and bring to boil.

Reduce heat to low, add kombu and continue cooking covered for a minimum of 3 hours – the longer it cooks, the thicker it will get. Add water as desired to thin, particularly when reheating leftovers. Remove bay leaf (if you can find it), season with salt and pepper to taste and serve. Soup will keep in refrigerator for up to 1 week or can be frozen in airtight containers.

VARIATION
Stir 1 teaspoon miso dissolved in 3 tablespoons water into each serving.

MAKES 8+ hearty servings

Sweet and Savory Root Vegetable Stew

I TAKE THE SAME APPROACH WITH THIS STEW as I do with my Goodness Soup *(page 208)* – I make it with whatever root vegetables I have on hand. Root vegetables are particularly strengthening, grounding and easy to digest, and they are abundant during the winter months. If you've shied away from them in the past because you didn't know how to cook them, this is a good place to start.

1	tablespoon extra virgin olive oil
6	shallots, diced
2	tablespoons grated fresh ginger
2	parsnips, peeled and diced
2	medium rutabagas, peeled and diced
2	turnips, peeled and diced
2	sweet potatoes, peeled and diced
1	celeriac (celery root), peeled and diced
1	fennel bulb, halved, cored and diced
1	cinnamon stick
	Vegetable stock
	Ume plum vinegar

In large pot over medium heat, sauté shallots and ginger in oil 5 minutes or until soft. Add parsnips, rutabagas, turnips, sweet potatoes, celery root, fennel and cinnamon stick. Add enough stock to barely cover vegetables, bring to boil, cover, reduce heat and simmer 25 minutes.

Remove from heat, discard cinnamon stick and gently purée soup 3 seconds using handheld blender to slightly thicken liquid and blend flavors. Season to taste with a few dashes of vinegar and serve.

SERVES 6–8

Super Strengthening Stew

MANY PEOPLE ASSOCIATE STRENGTH WITH PROTEIN, but too much protein can be dangerous. Root vegetables are particularly strengthening and can provide some of the sweetness that you may be craving – particularly if you've recently cut down on carbohydrates. From the purifying effects of burdock and rutabaga to the fat-dissolving ability of daikon and onion, this dish is packed with nutritional heavy hitters. Finishing the stew with a bit of soothing kudzu, you have a perfect winter meal.

1	strip kombu
1	tablespoon grapeseed oil
½	onion, diced
1	small yam
1	carrot
1	rutabaga
2	burdock roots
1	8-inch piece daikon
1	stalk celery, diced
2½	cups vegetable stock
⅛	teaspoon sea salt
1	head escarole, chopped
2	tablespoons kudzu
1	teaspoon toasted sesame oil

Gomasio for garnish

Place kombu in bowl with enough water to cover and soak 10 minutes or until soft. Drain, mince and set aside.

In Dutch oven over medium heat, sauté onion in grapeseed oil 3 minutes or until soft.

Peel and dice yam, carrot, rutabaga, burdock and daikon and add to pot along with celery and kombu. Add stock and salt, bring to boil, then reduce heat and simmer 10–15 minutes or until vegetables are soft. Fold in escarole, add water if needed to thin and simmer until esarole is soft.

In small cup, dissolve kudzu in 2 tablespoons water. Add to stew and stir 3–4 minutes or until liquid thickens. Remove from heat, drizzle with toasted sesame oil, garnish each serving with gomasio and serve.

SERVES 4

Three Bean Chili

MANY PEOPLE AVOID LEGUMES because of their unpleasant side effects. This chili, however, features smaller beans that are less gaseous and kombu, a sea vegetable that tenderizes and further reduces beans' gaseous properties. Black beans and aduki beans are particularly great for stabilizing blood sugar levels, so you can enjoy chili once again with nothing but benefits to your health.

1	thumb-size piece kombu
2	tablespoons extra virgin olive oil
3	garlic cloves, minced
2	onions, chopped
2	green bell peppers, diced
4	cups chopped tomatoes
½	cup tomato paste
¼	cup red wine
½	teaspoon dried oregano
1	teaspoon cumin
2	tablespoons chile powder
6–8	drops hot sauce
¼	teaspoon cayenne (or to taste)
¼	teaspoon sea salt
1½	cups cooked black beans
1½	cups cooked aduki beans
1½	cups cooked pinto beans
	Water or vegetable stock as needed
	Garnishes: chopped scallion, shredded soy or rice cheese, Tofu Sour Cream (page 101)

Place kombu in bowl with enough water to cover and soak 10 minutes or until soft. Drain, mince and set aside.

In large pot over medium heat, sauté garlic and onion in olive oil 3 minutes or until soft. Add green peppers and sauté 2 minutes more. Add chopped tomatoes and tomato paste, wine, oregano, cumin, chile powder, hot sauce, cayenne and salt. Add cooked beans and kombu, stir to combine and simmer at least 45 minutes. Add vegetable stock as needed to thin. Garnish as desired and serve.

SERVES 6

Tuscan Bean Soup

THIS SOUP HAS IT ALL – protein, calcium, minerals, and more! If you're short on time, use canned beans. For a heartier meal, serve over pasta or grilled polenta. Add some garlic bread and you have a delicious feast.

1	thumb-size piece kombu
2	tablespoons extra virgin olive oil
4	garlic cloves, minced
1	cup chopped onion
1	tablespoon dried basil
2	teaspoons dried oregano
¼	teaspoon dried rosemary
1½	cups cooked chickpeas
1½	cups cooked white beans
1½	cups cooked aduki beans
4	cups canned chopped tomatoes with their juices
1	bunch kale or collards, chopped into bite-size pieces
2	cups water or vegetable stock
1	tablespoon brown rice vinegar
1	cup red wine
Sea salt and freshly ground black pepper	
¼	cup chopped fresh parsley

Place kombu in bowl with enough water to cover and soak 10 minutes or until soft. Drain, mince and set aside.

In Dutch oven over medium heat, sauté garlic and onion in olive oil 3 minutes or until soft. Add basil, oregano and rosemary and stir. Add chickpeas, white beans, aduki beans, tomatoes, greens, kombu and stock or water. Bring to boil, then reduce heat and simmer. Stir in vinegar and wine, season with salt and pepper to taste, cover and cook for 45 minutes. Remove from heat, garnish with parsley and serve.

SERVES 6

Winter Squash and Aduki Bean Soup

ADUKI BEANS ADD A DELICIOUS TANG AND BALANCE to this otherwise sweet soup. They are one of the easiest legumes to digest and are particularly healing to the kidneys. Serve this soup with pan-roasted millet (*page 14*) and sautéed collard greens for color and balance.

1	thumb-size piece kombu
2	tablespoons extra virgin olive oil
1	large onion, chopped
2	stalks celery, diced
¼	teaspoon ground cumin
½	teaspoon ground cardamom
¼	teaspoon ground nutmeg
1	large butternut squash
1	cup apple cider
¼	cup mirin

Water or vegetable stock

3	cups cooked aduki beans
1	tablespoon apple cider vinegar

Sea salt and white pepper

Chopped scallions and/or fresh mint leaves for garnish

Place kombu in bowl with enough water to cover and soak 10 minutes or until soft. Drain, mince and set aside.

In large pot over medium heat, sauté onion and celery in olive oil 3 minutes or until soft. Add cumin, cardamom and nutmeg and stir. Peel and halve squash, remove seeds, cut into 1-inch chunks and add to pot along with cider, mirin and minced kombu. Add enough water or stock to cover squash. Cover pot and bring to boil. Reduce heat and simmer 45 minutes or until squash is tender.

Remove soup from heat and purée until smooth using handheld blender. Add cooked beans and vinegar, and season to taste with salt and white pepper. Return to low heat and simmer 10 minutes to blend flavors. Remove from heat, garnish as desired and serve.

SERVES 6

Spicy Coconut Pumpkin Soup

I LOVE TAKING THE FIRST SPOONFUL OF THIS SOUP and tasting the unexpected. You may need to make a trip to your local Asian grocery store to find some of these unusual ingredients, but it will be worth the effort. I often use butternut squash instead of pumpkin, as it has more flesh. Sugar pumpkins and red kuri squash are other tasty options. If using canned pumpkin, reduce your water or stock by 1 to 2 cups, and if you can't find galangal, subsitute ginger root.

---

2   tablespoons grapeseed oil

3   garlic cloves, minced

1   large onion, chopped

1   tablespoon grated fresh ginger

1   large butternut squash, peeled, halved, seeded and cubed

2   cups coconut milk

5   cups water or vegetable stock

6   lemongrass stalks (bottom 5 inches only), chopped

1   1-inch piece of galangal, peeled and chopped

4–5 dried Thai chiles, quartered

4   kaffir lime leaves, chopped

¼   cup chopped scallions

In soup pot or Dutch oven over medium heat, sauté garlic, onion and ginger in 1 tablespoon grapeseed oil until soft. Add squash, coconut milk, and water or stock. Bring to boil, then cover, reduce heat and simmer 15–20 minutes or until squash is soft.

Meanwhile, in small skillet over medium heat, sauté chopped lemongrass, galangal and chiles in remaining tablespoon of grapeseed oil until lightly browned. Remove from heat and set aside.

Using handheld blender, purée soup until smooth. Stir in lemongrass mixture and kaffir leaves. Simmer 15 minutes to infuse soup with spices. Pour through a mesh strainer and serve topped with chopped scallions.

SERVES 8

Winter Vegetable Soup

THIS EASY-TO-MAKE CABBAGE SOUP COOKS UP QUICKLY, but tastes like you spent hours fussing over it. It is a sweet and nutritious addition to any meal and makes a great midday snack.

---

1   tablespoon extra virgin olive oil

2   leeks (white and light green parts only), diced

3   tablespoons tamari

2   tablespoons mirin

1   large potato, peeled and diced

3   large carrots, diced

½   green cabbage, diced

2   stalks celery, diced

1   teaspoon sea salt

Freshly ground black pepper

Water or vegetable stock

2   cups corn, fresh or frozen

In large Dutch oven over medium heat, sauté leeks in olive oil, tamari and mirin until tender (about 5 minutes). Add potato, carrots, cabbage, celery, salt, and pepper to taste. Stir to combine and add enough water or stock to come ½-inch below top of vegetables. Bring to boil, then cover, reduce heat and simmer 20 minutes or until vegetables are soft. Remove from heat and purée using handheld blender. Add corn, adjust seasoning with salt and pepper and serve.

SERVES 6

Winter Green Salad with Sugared Walnuts, Crispy Pears and Pomegranate

THIS RECIPE COMBINES CRISP AND REFRESHING greens and pears with sweet and savory walnuts for a salad that is beautiful whether you serve it tossed in a large bowl or composed in individual servings. Substitute toasted and salted pumpkin seeds for the sugared walnuts for an equally satisfying variation.

---

6 cups chopped or torn bitter greens (arugula, romaine lettuce, frisée, dandelion greens or watercress)

2 D'Anjou pears (red or green), thinly sliced

Seeds from ½ pomegranate

SUGARED WALNUTS

1 tablespoon maple syrup

1 tablespoon walnut oil

1 tablespoon maple sugar

1 teaspoon ground cinnamon

2 cups walnuts

POMEGRANATE VINAIGRETTE

See recipe on page 201

Prepare vinaigrette, cover and refrigerate until ready to use.

PREPARING WALNUTS

Preheat oven to 350°F. In medium bowl, combine syrup, walnut oil, maple sugar and cinnamon. Add walnuts, toss to coat and spread on parchment-lined cookie sheet. Bake until lightly browned (about 20 minutes). Remove from oven and set aside.

ASSEMBLING

Place greens in salad bowl, combine with most (but not all) of the sliced pears, drizzle with pomegranate vinaigrette and toss to coat. Arrange remaining pears and sugared walnuts over salad greens, top with pomegranate seeds and serve.

SERVES 6

Bok Choy and Mung Bean Sprout Sauté with Peanuts and Scallions

MUNG BEANS ARE PARTICULARLY COOLING, cleansing and beneficial to the heart. When buying them, be sure to check the freshness date on the bag and look for firm white sprouts that don't have brown, dried ends. Buy sprouts just before you're ready to use them, as they will not last long, and wash them well before adding them to your recipe.

---

2 tablespoons extra virgin olive oil

3 garlic cloves, minced

1 tablespoon grated fresh ginger

1 large leek, thinly sliced

½ pound shiitake mushroom caps, thinly sliced

3 tablespoons tamari

2 tablespoons mirin

8 cups chopped bok choy (4 medium heads)

1 cup chopped scallions

2 cups mung bean sprouts, rinsed well

1½ cups dry-roasted peanuts

In large Dutch oven over medium heat, sauté garlic, ginger and leek in olive oil 5 minutes or until tender. Add shiitake mushrooms, half the tamari and mirin and sauté 5 minutes or until mushrooms start to caramelize. Add water 1 tablespoon at a time to deglaze pan as needed and continue sautéing mushrooms. Add remaining tamari and mirin and sauté another 3–4 minutes until mushrooms are glazed deep brown, but not burnt.

Stir in bok choy 2 cups at a time until it wilts and all fits in pot. Add water as needed to prevent sticking, cover and steam 1 minute. Remove cover, fold in scallions and cook 1 more minute. Remove from heat, fold in bean sprouts, top with peanuts and serve.

SERVES 6

Collard Greens and Black-Eyed Peas

THIS SOUTHERN DISH IS TRADITIONALLY EATEN on New Year's to ensure good luck and prosperity in the year ahead. I could give you more reasons to include this recipe in your diet, but I think this tradition speaks volumes. So don't question, just do it! What have you got to lose?

1 large bunch collard greens
2 tablespoons extra virgin olive oil
2 garlic cloves, minced
½ onion, diced
1½ cups cooked black-eyed peas
Dash of apple cider vinegar
Sea salt and freshly ground black pepper

Remove dry ends from collard green stems and chop leaves into bite-size pieces.

In large Dutch oven over medium heat, sauté garlic and onion in olive oil until soft. Add collard greens and stir until they turn bright green and wilt. Add water 1 tablespoon at a time as needed to keep greens from burning.

Add black-eyed peas and vinegar and continue cooking for 3–4 minutes to heat through. Season to taste with salt and pepper and serve.

SERVES 6

Shiitake Mushrooms and Bitter Greens in Filo

FILO HAS THE MAGICAL POWER of turning a simple dish into a sensation! Make small triangles to serve as an appetizer or side dish, or larger pockets to make into a main dish.

---

2 tablespoons grapeseed oil

4 garlic cloves, minced

1 large red onion, diced

20 shiitake mushroom caps, thinly sliced

2 tablespoons mirin

4 cups chopped bitter leafy greens (collards, kale, mustard greens or dandelion greens)

Sea salt and freshly ground black pepper

1 package filo dough (at least 9 sheets)

Extra virgin olive oil

PREPARING FILLING

In large sauté pan over medium heat, sauté garlic and onion in grapeseed oil until soft. Add mushrooms and sauté 5 minutes. Stir in mirin and greens, cover and cook 5 minutes or until greens wilt and turn bright green. Season with salt and pepper to taste and set aside to cool.

ASSEMBLING FILO POCKETS

Preheat oven to 350°F.

Defrost filo according to directions on package. On dry surface, lay out 2 sheets of filo – one on top of the other. Brush or spray lightly with olive oil, top with one more sheet of filo and again brush or spray with oil. Cut sheets from top to bottom into 4 strips.

Gently scoop out mushroom and greens mixture, draining excess liquid from each scoop, and place along edge of filo closest to you at the bottom of each strip. Fold bottom corner up and over greens to opposite edge and continue folding, flag-style, until you reach the top of each strip. Continue this process until all greens are used up. Wrap remaining filo and immediately return it to the freezer. Gently place pockets on parchment-lined cookie sheet, brush or spray lightly with olive oil and bake 25 minutes or until filo is golden brown and flaky.

VARIATION

Layer 3 sheets of filo and place filling along the bottom edge, leaving 3 inches on either side. Fold in sides and then roll filo into the shape of a log. Brush or spray with olive oil and bake as above.

SERVES 6

Roasted Brussels Sprouts with Fennel and Shiitake Mushrooms

ROASTING BRUSSELS SPROUTS CHANGES their dense texture and makes them soft and delicious, particularly when combined with these other caramelized vegetables. Brussels sprouts are a rich source of antioxidants and are desirable for their antibiotic and antiviral properties.

1½ pounds Brussels sprouts

4 shallots, quartered

10 garlic cloves, peeled

½ pound shiitake mushroom caps

1 large fennel bulb

¼ cup extra virgin olive oil

3 tablespoons balsamic vinegar

2 tablespoons fresh tarragon or rosemary

Coarse sea salt and freshly ground black pepper

Preheat to 425°F.

Prepare Brussels sprouts by cutting away tough root ends and removing any blemished outer leaves. Slice in half through the base and place in large bowl. Add shallots, garlic and mushroom caps.

Prepare fennel by trimming off dried root end and slicing bulb thinly widthwise. Add to vegetables and toss with olive oil, vinegar, tarragon, and salt and pepper to taste. Place in 9 x 12-inch glass or ceramic baking dish and roast uncovered 25 minutes. Stir vegetables and roast 25 minutes more. Remove from oven and serve.

SERVES 6

Not Mashed Potatoes

GETTING HEALTHY FOODS INTO OUR CHILDREN can be a challenge, and healthy additions like this one can be a mother's best friend. For years, my children had no idea that their mashed potatoes were half parsnips. They were happy because they were sweet and delicious, and I was happy because they were full of nutritional value. Whether you're adding powdered kelp to a smoothie or parsnips to your mashed potatoes, adults and children alike benefit from improving the nutrition of everyday foods.

2	medium baking potatoes
5	parsnips
¼	cup rice milk
2	tablespoons extra virgin olive oil
Sea salt	

Peel potatoes and parsnips. Cut into chunks and place in pot with 1–2 inches water. Cover and bring to boil. Cook until vegetables are soft – adding more water if needed. Drain remaining water into bowl and set aside. Add rice milk and olive oil to potatoes and parsnips and process with handheld blender until smooth. If too thick, add cooking water to thin. Season to taste with salt and process to the desired consistency. Serve hot.

SERVES 4

Sweet Potato and Parsnip Pancakes

THESE SWEET LITTLE PANCAKES ARE PERFECT with applesauce, maple syrup or even just a touch of sea salt. This is a great time to learn how to use the grating attachment on your food processor.

---

2   tablespoons ground golden flax seeds

1   large onion

3   parsnips, peeled

2   sweet potatoes, peeled

2   tablespoons mirin

½   cup cornmeal

Sea salt and freshly ground black pepper

Grapeseed oil for frying

Soak ground flax seeds for 10 minutes in bowl with ½ cup water.

Use the grating disc on your food processor to grate onion, parsnips and sweet potatoes. Place grated vegetables in large bowl. Add mirin and soaked flax. Sprinkle with cornmeal, salt and pepper to taste and combine. (I find that my hands do the best job.)

Preheat oven to 250°F.

Heat skillet or griddle over medium-high heat and add enough grapeseed oil to coat the bottom of the pan. Again using your hands, scoop out potato mixture, form into small balls, place in skillet and press flat with spatula to form pancakes. Fry pancakes 2–3 minutes on each side until golden brown and crisp. Remove from skillet and keep in warm oven while frying remaining batches, adding oil to skillet as needed. Serve hot.

MAKES 20 pancakes

Tree of Life Stir-Fry

THIS STIR-FRY GETS ITS NAME from the combination of broccoli and cauliflower, as well as the addition of strengthening and toning vegetables such as carrots, onions and arame. Ginger provides heat and energy to your core for healing. All together, this dish overflows with calcium, vitamins, antioxidants and beta-carotene.

1 cup dried arame

1 tablespoon grapeseed oil

1 small onion, cut into wedges

3 carrots, cut into matchsticks

1 small head broccoli, cut into bite-size pieces

½ head cauliflower, cut into bite-size pieces

1 tablespoon mirin

Water as needed

2 teaspoons kudzu dissolved in ¼ cup water

1 tablespoon mellow white or chickpea miso

1 tablespoon agave nectar

1 tablespoon grated fresh ginger

¼ cup toasted sesame seeds

Place arame in bowl with enough water to cover. Soak 10 minutes, drain and set aside.

In large skillet over medium heat, sauté onion in grapeseed oil 3 minutes until soft. Add carrots, broccoli, cauliflower and mirin and continue to stir-fry until vegetables become brighter in color. Drain arame and add to stir-fry, adding water as needed to prevent sticking.

In small bowl, combine dissolved kudzu with miso, agave and ginger. Add to stir-fry and cook 3–4 minutes to thicken sauce. Remove from heat, top with sesame seeds and serve.

SERVES 4

Butternut Squash Casserole

ONE WAY TO WARD OFF SWEET CRAVINGS is to add more nutritional sweetness to your diet. Winter squash is a delicious "sweet" and I particularly like this recipe, as it's easy to prepare and can be made in advance. Your guests will be overtaken by the wonderful aroma when they enter your home and will be even more impressed when you serve this satisfying dish.

1	small butternut squash, peeled, halved, seeded and thinly sliced
1	small red onion, thinly sliced
⅓	cup apple cider or juice
2	tablespoons grapeseed oil
2	tablespoons maple syrup
¼	cup toasted slivered almonds

Preheat oven to 350°F.

Combine squash and onion in 9 x 12-inch casserole. In small bowl, whisk together apple cider, oil and syrup. Pour over squash, top with almonds, cover with foil and bake 45 minutes or until tender.

SERVES 6

Winter Squash and Chestnut Casserole

FOR A WARMING AND SATISFYING DISH, try this combination of winter squash, rich and creamy chestnuts and crunchy nut topping. Chestnuts are often only sold around the holidays, so keep your eye out for when they go on sale in early January and stock up so you can enjoy this recipe throughout the winter.

---

1   small butternut squash, peeled, halved, seeded and cubed

2   cups cooked chestnuts

3   cups apple cider or juice

1   teaspoon ground cinnamon

½   teaspoon ground nutmeg

Pinch of ground cloves

½   cup toasted almonds, coarsely chopped

3   tablespoons brown rice syrup

½   teaspoon vanilla extract

Place squash, chestnuts, apple cider and spices in large pot. Bring to boil, cover, reduce heat and simmer 20–25 minutes until squash is soft. Remove from heat and purée with handheld blender until smooth. Spoon into an 8 x 8-inch baking dish and sprinkle with chopped nuts.

Set oven to broil.

In small pan over low heat, stir rice syrup to heat and thin. Remove from heat, stir in vanilla and drizzle over nut topping. Place baking dish under broiler for 3 minutes, but keep a close eye to make sure it doesn't burn. Remove from oven and serve.

SERVES 6

Simply Delicious Spaghetti Squash

SPAGHETTI SQUASH IS LESS SWEET than other winter squash varieties. It has a beautiful golden color and slightly crisp texture. Try it by itself or topped with your favorite pasta sauce. This recipe is a perfect complement to Sautéed Garlic Greens *(page 266)*.

---

1   spaghetti squash

¼   cup extra virgin olive oil

3   garlic cloves, minced

2   tablespoons chopped
     fresh parsley

Coarse sea salt and freshly
     black ground pepper

Preheat oven to 400°F.

Place squash on cookie sheet and bake 1 hour or until soft. Remove from oven and set aside.

In small skillet over low heat, sauté garlic in olive oil until soft (about 2 minutes). Cut squash in half lengthwise and remove and discard seeds. Hold half of the squash over a serving bowl and using a fork, scrape out flesh from top to bottom to separate the strands of squash. Repeat with other half, toss with garlic oil, parsley, and salt and pepper to taste. Serve hot.

SERVES 4

Roasted Kabocha Squash with Kale

THESE TWO WINTER STAPLES COMBINE to make an alkalinizing dish that's big in color, texture and taste.

1	small kabocha squash
4	shallots, quartered
3	tablespoons balsamic vinegar
3	tablespoons extra virgin olive oil
1	teaspoon coarse sea salt
2	garlic cloves, minced
2	bunches kale, chopped

Preheat oven to 425°F.

Leaving the skin on, cut squash in half, remove seeds and chop into bite-size pieces. In large bowl, combine squash with shallots, vinegar, 2 tablespoons olive oil and salt. Spread out onto cookie sheet and roast 30 minutes or until soft. Remove from oven and set aside.

Heat remaining tablespoon of oil in Dutch oven over medium heat. Sauté garlic until fragrant (about 2 minutes). Fold in kale a little at a time until it all fits in pot and cook until tender, adding water as needed to prevent burning. Remove from heat, add roasted squash, toss to evenly distribute and serve.

SERVES 6

Chestnut Stuffing

THIS STUFFING FEATURES RICE BREAD, which is slightly heavier than other breads and has a sourness similar to sourdough. Rice bread also has no gluten, making it perfect for the wheat-sensitive members of my family. Look for rice bread in the freezer section of your natural foods store. For an extra-special presentation, roast a hubbard squash, fill it with the stuffing and bake. To serve, scoop out the stuffing along with some squash. Yum!

---

3 tablespoons extra virgin olive oil

1 large yellow onion, diced

5 stalks celery, diced

½ pound cremini mushrooms, diced

½ cup diced dried apples

2 tablespoons chopped fresh rosemary

2 tablespoons dried parsley

2½ cups cooked chestnuts, diced

6 slices brown rice bread, cut into ½-inch cubes and toasted

½ cup vegetable stock

¼ cup tamari

2 tablespoons mirin

Freshly ground black pepper

½ cup toasted slivered almonds

Chopped fresh parsley for garnish

Preheat oven to 400°F.

In large Dutch oven over medium heat, sauté onion in olive oil until soft. Add celery, mushrooms, apples, rosemary and dried parsley and sauté 4 minutes. Fold in chestnuts and toasted bread cubes and remove from heat.

In small bowl, whisk together stock, tamari and mirin. Drizzle over stuffing mixture to evenly soak. Season with pepper to taste and gently fold to combine all ingredients. Place in large casserole or stuff into roasted winter squash and bake 25 minutes until top is lightly toasted.

Remove from oven, top with almonds and fresh parsley and serve.

SERVES 6

Arame with Caramelized Shiitakes

ARAME IS A RICH SOURCE of easily absorbable calcium and iron, is a powerful detoxifier, helps soften tissue masses, benefits the thyroid and supports hormone functions. Combined with shiitake mushrooms – known for their ability to lower blood cholesterol and regulate blood pressure – this recipe is definitely a nutritional heavy hitter!

1   cup dried arame
2   tablespoons grapeseed oil
12   shiitake mushroom caps, thinly sliced
2   tablespoons tamari
3–4 shallots, thinly sliced
2   carrots, shredded
1   3-inch piece daikon, peeled and cut into matchsticks
2   tablespoons mirin
2   tablespoons toasted sesame seeds
Toasted sesame oil
Sea salt

Place arame in bowl and fill with enough water to cover. Soak 10 minutes, rinse, drain and set aside.

In large skillet over medium heat, sauté shiitakes in grapeseed oil 10 minutes. If pan starts to stick, deglaze with 1 tablespoon tamari or water and continue stirring. Even if mushrooms appear done, make sure to sauté the full time to bring out their richness and caramelized taste and texture. Remove from heat and place in separate bowl. Return skillet to stovetop.

Heat remaining 1 tablespoon grapeseed oil in skillet and sauté shallots 3 minutes. Add carrots, daikon, mirin and remaining tablespoon tamari and sauté another 2–3 minutes. Add shiitakes and arame and heat through. Toss with toasted sesame seeds. Season to taste with sesame oil and sea salt and serve.

MAKES 6 servings

Savory "Unbaked" Beans

FOR A QUICK MEAL, there's nothing like canned beans. Eden makes theirs with kombu, so I always keep a few cans in my pantry. I make this meal when I have leftover brown rice. Simply reheat the rice in a pan with a bit of water, sauté some greens and heat the canned beans with your favorite seasonings. For a change, serve the beans and rice in soft tortillas with chopped lettuce and tomatoes. Either way, this is a 10-minute meal that my family loves!

1½ cups cooked black beans

1½ cups cooked aduki beans

1   tablespoon tahini

1   tablespoon molasses

1   tablespoon apple butter

1   tablespoon prepared mustard

2   tablespoons maple syrup

½   teaspoon ground cinnamon

½   teaspoon ground cumin

Hot pepper sauce

Drain and rinse canned beans and place in medium pot over medium heat. Add all other ingredients, stir to combine, cook to heat through and serve.

SERVES 4

Thai Black Beans with Mangoes and Cilantro

USED TRADITIONALLY IN THAI FOOD, fermented black beans taste like dried and salted black beans. They give this dish a strong savory flavor that complements the sweet mango and fresh cilantro, and provides welcome warmth during the cold months of winter.

¼ cup fermented black beans

2 garlic cloves, peeled

1 tablespoon grated fresh ginger

1 teaspoon roasted red chili paste

2 teaspoons toasted sesame oil

1 tablespoon sucanat

1 tablespoon lime juice

4 cups cooked black beans

2 mangoes, peeled, pitted and diced

½ cup coarsely chopped cilantro

Soak fermented black beans for 2 minutes in bowl with enough hot water to cover. Drain, rinse and drain again. Add garlic, ginger, chili paste, sesame oil, sucanat and lime juice. With handheld blender, mix to combine and set aside.

Heat cooked black beans in pot over medium heat for 4 minutes. Add fermented black bean sauce and stir continuously to combine and heat through. Using a rounded glass or stainless steel serving bowl as a mold, press in bean mixture, invert over the center of your serving dish, then remove mold. In separate bowl, combine mangoes and cilantro. Spoon mixture around black beans and serve.

SERVES 6

Lentil Apple Walnut Loaf

THIS HIGH-PROTEIN LOAF MAKES a nice main course for a vegetarian meal and a great sandwich stuffer as leftovers. Serve with Cranberry Applesauce *(page 205)* and sautéed greens *(pages 266–267)* for a complete meal.

1	cup dried lentils
3	cups vegetable stock
1	thumb-size piece kombu
3	tablespoons ground golden flax seed
½	cup water
3	tablespoons extra virgin olive oil
1	large yellow onion, diced
1	carrot, grated
1	stalk celery, minced
2	tablespoons mirin
1	apple, peeled, grated and mixed with 1 tablespoon lemon juice
¼	cup raisins
¾	cup toasted walnuts, chopped
1	teaspoon dried thyme
6–7	dashes ume plum vinegar
Freshly ground black pepper	
1	cup breadcrumbs

GLAZE

2	tablespoons ketchup
1	tablespoon balsamic vinegar
1	tablespoon maple syrup
1	tablespoon apple butter
1	tablespoon arrowroot

PREPARING LENTILS

Rinse lentils, place in rice cooker or pot and add stock and kombu. Bring to boil then reduce heat and simmer until liquid is absorbed and lentils are tender. Remove from heat, discard kombu and set aside.

PREPARING LOAF

In small bowl, combine ground flax seed with water and set aside.

Preheat oven to 350°F.

In large skillet over medium heat, sauté onion, carrot and celery in olive oil for 2 minutes. Add mirin and sauté 3 minutes more until soft. Add grated apple, raisins and walnuts and sauté another minute. Add thyme, vinegar, and pepper to taste. Remove from heat and fold in cooked lentils, breadcrumbs and soaked flax seed until evenly distributed. Press mixture firmly into lightly oiled loaf pan and set aside.

PREPARING GLAZE

In small saucepan over no heat, combine all glaze ingredients. Place over medium heat and stir continuously until thick (about 2–3 minutes). Spread evenly over loaf and bake, uncovered, 40 minutes. Remove from oven and serve.

Note: To make this recipe gluten-free, substitute brown rice breadcrumbs.

SERVES 6

Orange Ginger Tofu

I FIRST DISCOVERED TOFU ON A SALAD BAR. I took one bite into the mysterious, cold, bland cube and vowed never to eat it again! When I realized that tofu would take on the flavor of whatever I cooked it with, I changed my mind. I started adding it to recipes like my Tofu Kale Lasagna *(page 179)*, and roasting it with herbs, spices and marinades as I do here. If you've ever wondered what to do with tofu, this recipe is a great place to start. It's quick and easy and yields a sweet and savory tofu that complements everything from greens and winter squash to stir-fries and salads.

---

16 ounces firm tofu

MARINADE

2 tablespoons grated fresh ginger

3 garlic cloves, minced

3 tablespoons minced red onion

1 cup orange juice

¼ cup brown rice vinegar

¼ cup tamari

2 tablespoons toasted sesame oil

2 tablespoons maple syrup

Wrap tofu in towels and press to remove excess liquid. Cut lengthwise into 4 rectangular slices and then into cubes. In shallow baking dish, combine all marinade ingredients. Add tofu in a single layer and turn pieces to completely coat. Cover and refrigerate at least 30 minutes.

Preheat oven to 350°F.

Uncover tofu and bake in marinade 15 minutes. Turn pieces and bake another 15–20 minutes or until golden brown. Serve hot or chilled.

SERVES 4

Roasted Tofu with Green Beans

MY FRIEND JERILYN MADE THIS RECIPE FOR ME years ago, and it instantly became a winter favorite. Roasting is a great way to dress up basic tofu, and this recipe lends itself to improvisation. Make it your own by experimenting with asparagus, onion, fennel or Brussels sprouts. For a heartier meal, serve this dish over brown rice.

2	pounds fresh firm tofu (not silken), cut into cubes
10	garlic cloves, peeled
2	pounds green beans, dried ends removed
½	pound cremini mushrooms, stems removed
2	leeks
3	tablespoons extra virgin olive oil
¼	cup Bragg Liquid Aminos
All-purpose seasoning blend	

Preheat oven to 375°F.

Place tofu, garlic, green beans and mushrooms in 9 x 12-inch baking pan. Cut leeks in half lengthwise, rinse, cut into ¼-inch slices and add to pan. Drizzle olive oil and liquid aminos over tofu mixture, sprinkle generously with seasoning blend and toss to combine. Roast uncovered 1 hour, stirring every 20 minutes, until tofu is firm and vegetables are carmelized. Remove from oven and serve.

SERVES 4

Pad Thai with Tofu

I FELL IN LOVE WITH PAD THAI at a small restaurant outside Boston and spent years trying to re-create it. This version features roasted tofu instead of the traditional eggs. The tofu can be prepared up to a day in advance or can be left out if time is limited.

½ pound fettuccine-style rice noodles

Cook noodles according to directions on package. Drain and let sit in cold water. Drain just before using.

TOFU

½ pound fresh firm tofu (not silken)

½ cup Bragg Liquid Aminos

½ cup water

2 tablespoons mirin

PREPARING TOFU

Cut tofu into ¼-inch slices and place in shallow tray. In separate bowl, combine liquid aminos, water and mirin. Pour over tofu and marinate 30 minutes.

Preheat oven to 375°F. Place marinated tofu on cookie sheet and roast 15 minutes. Turn pieces over and roast 15 minutes longer or until firm. Remove from oven and cut into uneven 1-inch pieces.

STIR-FRY SAUCE

1 teaspoon roasted red chili paste

1 tablespoon sucanat

1 tablespoon tamari

1 tablespoon lime juice

½ cup water

PREPARING SAUCE

In small bowl, whisk together all sauce ingredients until chili paste and sucanat are dissolved. Set aside.

FINISHING STIR-FRY

In large sauté pan or wok, sauté garlic in oil 1 minute. Add stir-fry sauce and cook until it starts to thicken. Add tofu and snow peas and stir another minute. Add noodles and sauté 2–3 minutes to heat through. Remove from heat and stir in bean sprouts, cilantro, scallions and lime juice. Top with peanuts and serve.

SERVES 4

STIR-FRY

1 tablespoon grapeseed oil

3 garlic cloves, minced

½ cup thinly sliced snow peas

1½ cups mung bean sprouts, rinsed well

3 tablespoons chopped fresh cilantro

4 scallions, thinly sliced

Juice of 1 lime

½ cup dry roasted peanuts

Spicy Thai Tempeh with Cashews

MY HUSBAND LIKES NEARLY EVERYTHING that comes out of my kitchen, but tempeh is the one food he refused, hands down. I only wish I had had my video camera when he tasted this dish and loved it. Since then, I've converted many more non-tempeh eaters into tempeh lovers. We serve this dish with Zesty Basmati Rice with Cinnamon and Cumin *(page 241)* and steamed bok choy or pac choy.

---

1   8-ounce package tempeh
1   tablespoon extra virgin olive oil
1   red onion, diced
1   roasted red bell pepper, diced
1   cup toasted cashews, chopped
1   tablespoon roasted red chili paste
2   tablespoons maple syrup
2   teaspoons tamari
⅓   cup water
4   scallions, finely chopped

Cut tempeh into large chunks and steam 8 minutes. Remove from heat and set aside until cool enough to handle.

In large cast-iron skillet or Dutch oven over medium heat, sauté onion in olive oil 10 minutes or until caramelized. Crumble chunks of tempeh directly into skillet. Add roasted red pepper and cashews and sauté 5 minutes.

In small bowl, whisk together chili paste, syrup, tamari and water. Pour over tempeh, and sauté another minute to combine flavors. Remove from heat, top with chopped scallions and serve.

SERVES 4

Sautéed Tempeh with Coconut Milk and Snow Peas

TEMPEH IS A WONDERFUL SOURCE of soy isoflavones, protein, vitamins and minerals. When steamed, it puffs up and is better able to absorb flavors from marinades and sauces. Serve this dish over basmati rice.

2	8-ounce packages of tempeh
1	cup snow peas
2	tablespoons grapeseed oil
2	garlic cloves, minced
1	tablespoon grated fresh ginger
½	cup golden raisins
½	cup coconut milk
2	tablespoons tamari
2	tablespoons maple syrup
1	tablespoon mirin
5	scallions, chopped
½	cup chopped fresh cilantro

Cut tempeh into bite-size chunks and steam 8 minutes. Remove from heat and set aside.

Trim snow peas and place in bowl. Bring 2 cups water to boil, pour over peas. Leave for 2 minutes then drain. Rinse with cool water and set aside.

In large skillet over medium heat, sauté garlic and ginger in grapeseed oil until soft (about 2 minutes). Add tempeh, raisins, coconut milk, tamari, syrup and mirin and cook 5 minutes or until tempeh starts to brown, adding water as needed to deglaze pan. Add snow peas and cook 2 minutes longer. Remove from heat, top tempeh with scallions and cilantro and serve.

SERVES 6

Seitan Shepherd's Pie

THIS HEARTY CASSEROLE IS VERY SATISFYING, whether you're vegan, a meat-and-potatoes lover or somewhere in between.

POTATO TOPPING

5–6 small russet potatoes, quartered

¼ cup rice milk

¼ teaspoon sea salt

2 tablespoons extra virgin olive oil

FILLING

16 ounces seitan

1 large portobello mushroom cap

1 tablespoon extra virgin olive oil

2 garlic cloves, minced

1 onion, chopped

½ teaspoon ground cumin

1 tablespoon dried basil

3 carrots, diced

½ cup corn, fresh or frozen

1 bunch kale or collards, chopped into bite-size pieces

¼ cup mirin

3 tablespoons tamari

1 cup vegetable stock mixed with 1 tablespoon kudzu

Sea salt and freshly ground black pepper

Paprika

PREPARING POTATOES

Place potatoes in pot with enough water to cover. Bring to boil and cook until easily pierced with fork (about 20 minutes). Drain cooking water, add rice milk, salt, and olive oil and mash until smooth and creamy. Set aside.

Preheat oven to 350°F.

PREPARING FILLING

Chop seitan and mushroom into large pieces, place together in food processor and process until coarse and crumbly.

In large pot or skillet over medium heat, sauté garlic and onion in olive oil until soft. Add seitan mushroom mixture, cumin and basil and cook 2–3 minutes. Add water as needed to prevent sticking. Add carrots, corn, kale, mirin, tamari and stock with kudzu. Stir to combine, cover and cook 5 minutes or until kale is tender and bright green. Season with salt and pepper to taste and pour into deep casserole.

FINISHING

Spread mashed potatoes over vegetable mixture and sprinkle with paprika. Bake uncovered 25–30 minutes until sauce starts to bubble. Remove from oven, cool slightly and serve.

SERVES 6

Seitan Bourguignon

THIS RICH DISH COMBINES RED WINE, wild mushrooms and seitan in a distinctive, aromatic and filling main dish that requires hearty accompaniments that can hold their own, such as basmati or wild rice *(page 14)* and Sautéed Garlic Greens *(page 266)* or Ginger Sesame Greens *(page 267)*.

2	tablespoons extra virgin olive oil
2	garlic cloves, minced
6	shallots, thinly sliced
1	pound cremini mushrooms, thinly sliced
1	pound shiitake mushroom caps, thinly sliced
2	stalks celery, minced
1	tablespoon finely chopped fresh rosemary
1	tablespoon fresh thyme leaves
2	teaspoons finely chopped fresh sage
3	tablespoons tamari
2	cups dry red wine
2	pounds seitan, sliced into thin strips
1	bay leaf
½	cup vegetable stock
2	tablespoons arrowroot
Freshly ground black pepper	
¼	cup chopped fresh parsley

In large skillet over medium heat, sauté garlic and shallots in olive oil until soft. Add cremini and shiitake mushrooms, celery, rosemary, thyme, sage, tamari and wine. Bring to simmer, add seitan and bay leaf, cover and cook 15 minutes until mushrooms are tender.

In small bowl, whisk together vegetable stock and arrowroot until arrowroot dissolves. Slowly pour into skillet and continue whisking until sauce starts to thicken. Turn off heat and discard bay leaf. Season to taste with pepper, top with parsley and serve.

SERVES 6

Wholegrain Pancakes

THIS GRAIN VERSION OF AN OLD FAVORITE, potato pancakes, is delicious served with maple syrup or applesauce and even a dash of cinnamon. Cooking grains in extra water will make them mushier, which helps them stick together. Experiment with different grains and amounts of water to find the texture you and your family like best. This is a great way to use up leftover grains.

---

1   cup uncooked or 2½–3 cups cooked grain (brown rice, millet and quinoa all work well)

1   thumb-size piece kombu

2¼ cups water

1   medium onion, finely chopped

½   cup grated raw carrot, sweet potato or winter squash

1   tablespoon extra virgin olive oil

Sea salt

¼   cup brown rice flour

Maple syrup or applesauce as topping (optional)

Rinse grain and place in rice cooker or large pot with kombu and water. Bring to boil, then reduce heat and simmer until liquid is absorbed and grain is soft. Remove from heat, discard kombu and set aside. If using refrigerated leftover grains, heat in skillet with ½ cup water and sauté 4–5 minutes.

Preheat oven to 350°F.

In large skillet over medium heat, sauté onion and grated carrot, sweet potato or squash in olive oil for 6-8 minutes or until very soft. Add grain, season to taste with salt and fold together. Add flour 1 tablespoon at a time and mix until everything sticks together. You may not need all of the flour. Remove from heat and set aside until cool enough to handle.

Using an ice cream scoop, form balls of grain mixture and place on parchment-lined cookie sheet. Flatten with fork to about ¼-inch thick. Bake 10 minutes, carefully flip pancakes and bake another 10 minutes. Serve with maple syrup or applesauce as desired.

SERVES 6

Zesty Basmati Rice with Cinnamon and Cumin

A SIMPLE YET DELICIOUS ACCOMPANIMENT to a variety of foods, such as sweet winter squash, sautéed Asian greens and warming Thai dishes.

1½ cups brown basmati rice

3 cups water or vegetable stock

1 cinnamon stick

½ teaspoon ground cumin

¼ teaspoon sea salt

Zest of 1 orange

1 tablespoon toasted sesame oil

½ cup toasted cashew pieces

½ cup coarsely chopped fresh cilantro or parsley

Soak rice for 1 hour in bowl with enough water to cover. Drain and place in rice cooker or large pot with water or stock, cinnamon stick, cumin, salt and orange zest. Bring to boil, cover, reduce heat and simmer until all water is absorbed (about 25 minutes). Remove from heat and discard cinnamon stick. Fluff with fork, toss with sesame oil, cashews and cilantro or parsley and serve.

SERVES 6

Sweet Brown Rice and Mung Beans with Indian Spices

HERBS, SPICES, LEGUMES AND VERY LITTLE EFFORT – that's all it takes to turn plain rice into something special! These Indian spices are warming to the body and especially comforting on a cold winter day.

¾ cup mung beans, soaked overnight in 4 cups water

¾ cup sweet brown rice

3 cups water

Pinch of sea salt

1 tablespoon grapeseed oil

1 large onion, diced

½ teaspoon ground cloves

½ teaspoon ground cinnamon

½ teaspoon ground cardamom

¼ teaspoon ground turmeric

Drain beans and rinse well.

Rinse rice and place in rice cooker or large pot. Add mung beans, water and salt. Bring to boil, cover, then reduce heat and simmer until water is absorbed and grains and beans are tender (about 45 minutes). Remove from heat and set aside to cool (fluffing too soon will yield mushy rice and beans).

In medium skillet over medium heat, sauté onion in oil until soft. Reduce heat to low, stir in cloves, cinnamon, cardamom and turmeric. Sauté another minute and remove pan from heat. Fluff rice and beans, gently fold in onion mixture and serve hot.

SERVES 6

Jasmine Rice with Sweet Peas

MANY RECIPES SUGGEST STEAMING JASMINE RICE in a double boiler or even wrapped in cheesecloth. I find that the heat in my rice cooker is indirect enough to turn out tender, fluffy jasmine rice every time. Be sure to follow the appropriate directions for the type of rice you are using (white or brown).

2	cups white jasmine rice or 1 cup brown jasmine rice
4	cups water
	Pinch of sea salt
1½	cups peas, fresh or frozen
2	tablespoons lemon juice
1	tablespoon grated lemon peel
2	tablespoons chopped fresh parsley

Rinse and drain rice 3–4 times until water runs clear. Place in rice cooker with 2 cups water and salt and cook until liquid is absorbed, about 15 minutes for white rice and 25 minutes for brown rice.

Place peas in strainer. Bring 2 cups water to boil and pour over peas to blanch or thaw. Fold in peas, lemon juice and lemon peel into cooked rice. Top with chopped parsley and serve.

SERVES 6

Millet with Cranberries and Pistachios

MILLET'S LIGHT FLAVOR MAKES IT A NICE ACCOMPANIMENT to winter squash, roasted nuts and dried fruit. It is high in protein and has no gluten. I like to pan-roast millet before cooking it to bring out its nutty flavor.

1½ cups millet

3 cups water

¾ cup dried cranberries

Pinch of sea salt

3 tablespoons extra virgin olive oil

4 dashes ume plum vinegar

¾ cup roasted pistachios, shelled

1 tablespoon chopped fresh parsley

Rinse and drain millet. Pan-roast in large skillet over medium heat for 3–4 minutes, until water evaporates and millet gives off a nutty aroma. Add water, dried cranberries and salt, stir and bring to boil. Cover, reduce heat to low and cook 25 minutes or until all water is absorbed. Remove from heat and set aside for 5 minutes.

Fluff millet with fork, drizzle with olive oil and vinegar and gently fold to combine. Top with pistachios and chopped parsley and serve.

SERVES 6

Polenta au Gratin

MADE FROM COARSELY GROUND CORN, polenta is a flavorful alternative to pasta. There are a variety of prepared polentas (both plain and seasoned) available in markets today that make this dish a breeze to throw together.

POLENTA

1 pound prepared polenta

1 tablespoon extra virgin olive oil

2 cups prepared pasta sauce

½ cup water

FILLING

1 tablespoon extra virgin olive oil

2 garlic cloves, minced

1 large red onion, thinly sliced

1 sprig fresh rosemary leaves, minced

1 cup thinly sliced cremini mushrooms

1 bunch Swiss chard, chopped

¼ cup grated soy or rice mozzarella or parmesan

Sea salt and freshly ground black pepper

Preheat oven to 350°F.

PREPARING POLENTA

Cut polenta into small pieces. Heat 1 tablespoon olive oil in large pot over medium heat. Add polenta and sauté 1 minute. Add 3 tablespoons pasta sauce and water and stir. Cover and cook 5 minutes or until polenta softens and falls apart. Cream polenta with fork, wooden spoon or handheld blender. Remove from heat, cover and set aside.

PREPARING FILLING

Heat 1 tablespoon olive oil in large skillet over medium heat. Add garlic, onion and rosemary and sauté until soft, adding water as needed to prevent sticking. Add mushrooms and chard. Cover and cook 3–4 minutes or until chard is soft. Season to taste with salt and pepper and remove from heat.

ASSEMBLING

Lightly oil 8 x 8-inch casserole and spread half the polenta evenly over the bottom. Cover with half the remaining pasta sauce, the chard mixture, the remaining polenta, pasta sauce and grated cheese. Cover with foil and bake for 15 minutes. Uncover and bake another 10 minutes. Remove from oven, let set 5 minutes and serve.

SERVES 6

Baked Stuffed Shells

MY OLDEST DAUGHTER IS A NUT FOR my Tofu Kale Lasagna *(page 179)*. This dish takes its key ingredients from the lasagna, but requires only half the time and effort and disappears every bit as quickly once it hits her plate!

---

8   ounces large pasta shells

3   tablespoons extra virgin olive oil

3   garlic cloves, minced

1   large onion, chopped

¼   cup mirin

2   teaspoons dried basil

2   teaspoons dried parsley

1½ pounds fresh firm tofu (not silken)

2   bunches kale or collard greens, chopped

Sea salt and freshly ground pepper

4   cups tomato sauce

1   cup grated soy or rice mozzarella

Preheat oven to 400°F.

Cook shells according to instructions on package, drain and set aside.

PREPARING FILLING

In large skillet or Dutch oven over medium heat, sauté garlic and onions in olive oil until soft (about 5 minutes). Add mirin, basil and parsley and stir. Wrap tofu in paper towels and press to remove excess liquid. Crumble tofu into pot, mix with other ingredients and cook 5 minutes.

Fold greens into tofu mixture and continue cooking until soft. Season to taste with salt and pepper, remove from heat and set aside until cool enough to handle.

ASSEMBLING

Stuff shells with filling and place in 9 x 12-inch lasagna pan. Cover stuffed shells with tomato sauce. Sprinkle top with cheese, cover with foil and bake 20 minutes. Remove foil and bake uncovered 10 minutes. Remove from oven and let set 5 minutes before serving.

SERVES 4

Maple-Spiced Almonds

I SERVE THESE AROMATIC NUTS AROUND THE HOLIDAYS and people devour them. They're also great sprinkled over a salad or granola or chopped and served over ice cream.

---

3   cups whole almonds

1   tablespoon canola or walnut oil

3   tablespoons maple syrup

2   tablespoons pumpkin pie spice

Preheat oven to 350°F.

In large bowl, whisk together oil, syrup and pumpkin pie spice. Add almonds and stir to coat. Spread almonds evenly on parchment-lined cookie sheet and bake until nuts start to brown, 20–25 minutes. Remove from oven and cool completely. Break nuts apart and store in airtight container.

MAKES 3 cups

Sinful Stuffed Dates

I USED TO MAKE THESE TREATS ON THE SLY. When the kids went to bed, I'd grab a date, slice it open and stuff it with some nuts, some chocolate chips…whatever I could get a hold of quickly! After much sneaking, I decided to admit my sins (OK, so I got caught) and turned my cheating into a legitimate – yet sinfully delicious – recipe.

---

18 dates
Zest of 1 orange
½ cup chopped pecans
¼ teaspoon ground cinnamon
½ cup + 2 tablespoons shredded dried unsweetened coconut
2 tablespoons maple syrup
1 tablespoon canola oil

Preheat oven to 350°F.

In small bowl, combine orange zest, chopped pecans, cinnamon, 2 tablespoons coconut, syrup and canola oil. Stir until evenly coated. Transfer to parchment-lined cookie sheet and roast 5–6 minutes until lightly browned. Remove from oven and set aside.

Carefully slice each date down one side and remove pit. If necessary, make small cuts in rounded ends of dates so they do not tear. Gently turn date inside out, placing sticky side down on work surface.

Press ¼ teaspoon roasted nut mixture into each date. Fold up edges and press seam and ends together to seal shut. Place remaining ½ cup coconut in small bowl, then press and roll sealed dates in coconut to coat. Arrange on tray and serve.

MAKES 18 dates

Sesame Almond Balls

THESE ALMOND BALLS ARE A PERFECT BITE-SIZE DESSERT. If you want something more to sink your teeth into, bake up some cinnamon-raisin mochi squares and stuff them with this mixture.

½ cup toasted sesame seeds

½ cup almond butter

¼ cup toasted sunflower seeds

¼ cup toasted almonds

4–5 dates, pitted

Place ¼ cup sesame seeds in small bowl and set aside.

In food processor, combine remaining ingredients and process to form a stiff paste or meal. Form into tablespoon-size balls and roll in reserved sesame seeds to coat. Serve immediately or store in airtight container for up to 4 days.

MAKES 12–15 balls

Coconut Cranberry Pecan Balls

THIS RECIPE WAS CREATED AT THE END OF A CLASS that did not include a dessert. The meal was a hit, but as soon as I served it, I felt desperate for something sweet. While everyone ate, I quickly pulled out my food processor and a couple of goodies from my cupboard, and this was the result. The lesson? If you put good ingredients in, you'll get a good result out!

¼   cup shredded dried unsweetened coconut

1½   cups toasted pecans

1   cup dried cranberries

½   cup almond butter

½   cup maple syrup

Place coconut in small bowl and set aside.

In food processor, combine remaining ingredients and process to form a stiff paste or meal. Form into tablespoon-size balls and roll in coconut to coat. Serve immediately or store in airtight container for up to 4 days.

MAKES 12–15 balls

Poached Winter Fruit Medley

THIS SIMPLE DESSERT WILL SATISFY your need for that little something sweet at the end of a meal, and you'll enjoy the added benefit of a home filled with the wonderful aroma of brewing spices. For an extra-special presentation, serve with vanilla bean ice cream and a sprig of mint.

1½ cups water

½ cup maple syrup

Zest of 1 orange

6 cloves

2 cinnamon sticks

½ teaspoon lemon extract

4 ripe but firm pears, peeled, cored and quartered

4 apples, peeled, cored and quartered

2 dried Calimyrna figs, quartered

¼ cup dried cranberries or cherries

Combine water, syrup, zest, cloves, cinnamon sticks and lemon extract in large pot over medium heat and bring to simmer. Place pears and apples in simmering syrup, reduce heat to medium-low and poach 10 minutes. Add figs and cranberries and cook another 10 minutes, or until fresh fruits are tender and syrup has reduced by half. Serve warm or chilled.

SERVES 4

Pear and Fig Tart in Pecan Crust

THIS NONTRADITIONAL TART is less sweet than many of my other desserts, makes an impressive presentation and has delicious rich flavor. Pair it with a scoop of vanilla bean ice cream and a glass of Port.

CRUST
2 cups pecans
1 cup brown rice flour
⅓ cup canola oil
⅓ cup brown rice syrup

FIG FILLING
10 dried Calimyrna figs
1 cup water
2 cups pear or apple juice
1 tablespoon agave nectar
1 tablespoon orange zest
2 tablespoons tapioca flour
½ teaspoon vanilla extract

TOPPING AND GLAZE
3 large D'Anjou pears
2 tablespoons lemon juice
1 cup pear or apple juice
1 tablespoon agave nectar
¼ teaspoon vanilla extract
2 teaspoons arrowroot

PREPARING CRUST
Preheat oven to 350°F. Place pecans in food processor and coarsely chop. Add brown rice flour and process briefly. Combine oil and brown rice syrup in small bowl, add to nut mixture and process until combined. Transfer to 11-inch tart pan and press to form crust. Pierce several times with fork and bake 12 minutes or until golden brown. Remove from oven and set on wire rack to cool.

PREPARING FILLING
Remove and discard tough ends of figs and cut figs into quarters. Place in pot with water and juice. Bring to boil, then reduce heat and simmer until figs are soft and 1½ cups of liquid remain (about 25 minutes). Remove from heat, add agave nectar and orange zest. Purée mixture with handheld blender until smooth. Gradually stir in tapioca flour and vanilla, pour into tart crust and spread evenly to cover bottom.

PREPARING PEARS
Peel, core and slice pears. Cut into equal-size thin, flat wedges and toss with lemon juice. Place in steamer basket and steam 3 minutes, or until just soft (oversteaming will make pears mushy). Remove steamer basket and cool pears. Arrange over fig filling in overlapping, fanlike pattern with ends pointing toward center of tart.

PREPARING GLAZE AND FINISHING
In small pan over no heat, combine apple or pear juice, agave nectar, vanilla and arrowroot. Place over medium heat and stir continuously until mixture thickens and becomes translucent. Spoon evenly over tart and refrigerate to set (about 1 hour). Serve cool.

SERVES 8

Chocolate Pecan Pie

WHEN IT COMES TO THANKSGIVING, PECAN PIE IS A MUST! This version – made without the traditional eggs, brown sugar and butter – is free of guilt but full of rich flavor and will have you eating pecan pie more than once a year.

CRUST

- 1½ cups almonds
- 1 cup rolled oats
- ¼ cup cocoa powder
- ¼ teaspoon sea salt
- ¼ cup walnut oil
- ¼ cup maple syrup

FILLING

- 2 tablespoons ground golden flax seeds
- 1 cup apple juice
- ½ cup raisins
- ½ cup honey
- ½ cup cocoa powder
- Pinch of sea salt
- 2 tablespoons cashew butter
- 1 teaspoon vanilla extract
- 2 cups lightly toasted pecans

Preheat oven to 350°F. Lightly oil 9-inch tart pan.

PREPARING CRUST

Place almonds, oats, cocoa and salt in food processor and process to form a crumb-like mixture. Add oil and syrup and process to combine. Place mixture in tart pan, press to form crust, pierce several times with fork and bake 12 minutes or until lightly browned. Remove from oven and cool on wire rack. Keep oven on.

PREPARING FILLING

Soak ground flax in bowl with 6 tablespoons water for 20 minutes. Meanwhile, in small pot, combine apple juice, raisins, honey, cocoa powder and salt. Place over medium heat and simmer for 10 minutes (raisins will lose their form). Add cashew butter to soaked flax seed mixture and whisk into apple juice mixture. Continue whisking until texture is uniform or purée gently with handheld blender. Remove from heat, stir in vanilla and set aside.

ASSEMBLING

Arrange 1½ cups toasted pecans over cooked pie crust. Pour in filling and arrange remaining pecans on top. Cover loosely with foil and bake 50 minutes. Remove from oven and place on wire rack to set. Serve at room temperature.

SERVES 10–12

Chestnut Cream Pie

PREPARED CHESTNUTS ARE A SEASONAL SPECIALTY ITEM that you will find on sale as soon as the holidays are over. I stock up on them so I can easily enjoy making this pie all winter long. Store-bought crust makes this simple pie whip up in a snap. Not overly sweet or indulgent, the smooth texture and pungent cinnamon in this pie satisfy even my most stubborn cravings.

---

1   9-inch prepared pie crust

TOPPING
1   teaspoon canola oil
1   teaspoon maple syrup
1   teaspoon ground cinnamon
1   cup coarsely chopped almonds

FILLING
2   cups prepared chestnuts
1   cup rice milk
2   teaspoons ground cinnamon
1½   teaspoons vanilla extract
Pinch of ground allspice
3   tablespoons agave nectar
2   tablespoons agar powder
½   cup apple juice

Preheat oven to 375°F.

Pierce pie crust 6–7 times and bake 20 minutes or until lightly browned. Remove from oven and cool on wire rack.

PREPARING TOPPING

In small bowl, combine oil, syrup and cinnamon. Add chopped almonds and toss to coat. Spread nuts on parchment-lined cookie sheet and bake 10 minutes or until browned. Remove from oven and set aside.

PREPARING FILLING

In food processor, combine chestnuts, rice milk, cinnamon, vanilla, allspice and agave until smooth.

In small pot over medium heat, whisk together agar powder and apple juice until powder dissolves and mixture thickens. Remove from heat, add to food processor and process briefly to combine.

FINISHING

Pour mixture into pie crust and top with spiced nuts. Refrigerate 1 hour to set. Serve cold or at room temperature.

SERVES 8

Tiramisu

TEFF FLOUR IS GREAT FOR BAKING WHEN YOU'RE AVOIDING GLUTEN, but it tends to yield a drier product than white or wheat flour. In this recipe, the cake gains moistness from the coffee syrup, but you still need to be careful not to overbake. To ensure a more moist cake, bake it a day in advance, cool completely, then cover and refrigerate until ready to serve.

CAKES

2	cups ivory teff flour
1	cup tapioca flour
¼	teaspoon sea salt
1½	tablespoons baking powder
1	teaspoon baking soda
½	cup canola oil
1	cup maple syrup
¼	cup rice milk
¼	cup apple juice
1	tablespoon vanilla extract

TOFU CREAM

See recipe on page 141

SYRUP

¾	cup hot grain coffee substitute or coffee of choice
¼	cup maple syrup
1	tablespoon vanilla extract
1	teaspoon almond extract

Cocoa powder for garnish

Preheat oven to 325°F.

PREPARING CAKES

Lightly oil 24 shallow muffin cups. In large bowl, combine flours, salt, baking powder and baking soda. In separate bowl, combine oil, syrup, rice milk, apple juice and vanilla. Pour wet ingredients into dry and whisk until just combined. Scoop 2 tablespoons of batter into each muffin cup and bake 8–10 minutes until tops are just browned and a toothpick inserted into center of muffin comes out clean. Remove from oven and place on wire rack to cool. Muffins will break if handled before completely cooled.

PREPARING TOFU CREAM AND SYRUP

Prepare tofu cream according to recipe on page 141. Make syrup in small bowl by whisking together coffee substitute, maple syrup, vanilla and almond extract.

ASSEMBLING

Remove muffins from tins and place 1 on each plate. Top with drizzled syrup, a scoop of cream, another muffin, more syrup and more cream. Sift cocoa over whole plate, repeat with remaining muffins, syrup and cream and serve.

SERVES 12

There is no season such delights can bring as
summer, autumn, winter and spring.

WILLIAM BROWNE

Anytime

It's a lofty intention to strive for conscious seasonal eating that nourishes mind, body and soul, that balances us with the environment and that intimately connects us to our communities and the earth. But let's face it, good health is served by much more than good nutrition! At times I am nourished as much by the activities around food as by the food itself: weekly trips to the farm, discovering new restaurants, making rice pudding with my children and more. There are staples that transcend the seasons — some come in the form of recipes while others come in the form of rituals. Perhaps it's because they are so simple, or because they are so simply delicious. At the end of the day, if there is any intention worth holding, it is to savor every bite, feed your relationships and that which connects you, and sauté up a healthy serving of love each and every day.

ANYTIME

Maple Nut Granola

THE KEY TO MAKING DELICIOUS GRANOLA is to bake it at a low temperature for a long time. Of course, a little bit of shredded coconut and a lot of cinnamon and maple syrup help, too! My husband devours this granola every morning and at the end of each week leaves the nearly empty Mason jar on the counter to remind me to make more.

4	cups rolled oats
2	cups crispy brown rice cereal
1	cup toasted sunflower seeds
1½	cups shredded dried unsweetened coconut
1	cup sliced almonds
½	cup pecans, cashews, or walnuts
1	cup raisins
2	tablespoons ground cinnamon
¾	cup canola oil
¾	cup maple syrup
1	teaspoon almond extract

Preheat oven to 250°F.

In large bowl, mix together all dry ingredients. In separate bowl, whisk together oil, syrup and almond extract. Pour wet mixture over dry and stir to coat. Transfer granola to 9 x 12-inch glass casserole, spread evenly and push raisins into granola so they are not on the surface. Place on top rack of oven and bake 60 minutes or until golden. Remove from oven and cool completely to set. When cool, slide spatula along bottom of casserole to release granola. Break into chunks, and store in airtight container.

MAKES 10 cups

Pita Chips

THESE CHIPS ARE DELICIOUS ON THEIR OWN and also make a perfect accompaniment to soups, bean dips, Muffaletto *(page 41)* or Olive Tapenade *(page 203)*. Season them any way you want for a variety of flavors.

6–8 small pita pockets

OPTION 1
Extra virgin olive oil
All-purpose seasoning blend

OPTION 2
Toasted sesame oil
Gomasio

Preheat oven to 350°F.

Split each pita into 2 rounds. Place rough side up on cookie sheet. Pour oil into small bowl and brush onto each pita. Sprinkle lightly with seasoning, cut into triangular wedges and bake 6–8 minutes or until lightly browned. Baking time will vary according to the thickness of pitas. Remove from oven, cool and serve. Store in airtight container.

VARIATIONS
Try seasoning chips with a combination of olive oil, ground mustard and garlic powder, or canola oil with pumpkin pie spice, curry, nutmeg or cinnamon. You're only limited by your own imagination!

Toasted Sesame Nori Crisps

MANY YEARS AGO I DISCOVERED SESAME NORI CRISPS at my local health food store. They came in a tiny deli-style container, and I devoured them in less than a minute. Even my kids couldn't get enough! Now I make them in huge batches, as they are always a welcome gift for family and friends. Serve nori crisps with any meal, save them for a nutritionally packed and satisfying snack or use them as a garnish for fish, grains or salads.

---

3 sheets toasted nori
½ cup canola oil
Cayenne
½ cup brown rice syrup
1½ cups sesame seeds
Spice of choice
    (nutmeg, cinnamon,
    pumpkin pie spice…)
Sea salt

Preheat oven to 350°F.

Stack nori sheets, cut into 2-inch strips, stack again and cut in half. Cover cookie sheet with parchment paper, and lay individual strips of nori side by side on paper. In small bowl, whisk together oil, syrup, and a pinch of cayenne.

Using a pastry brush, generously coat the top of each piece of nori with syrup mixture. Oil and syrup tend to separate, so continue to mix as you work. When all nori pieces are coated, sprinkle with sesame seeds, spice of choice and salt. Toast in oven 5–7 minutes – keep a close eye as they burn easily. When seeds are light brown, remove from oven and set aside to cool until nori is firm enough to handle. Flip nori pieces, brush with syrup mixture, sprinkle with sesame seeds, seasoning and salt. Return to the oven for another 5–7 minutes. Remove from oven and cool completely. Repeat until all ingredients are used up.

Store in airtight container.

Quick Homemade Pickles

MACROBIOTICS TEACHES US that pickles aid digestion and recommends serving them with every meal. This approach to pickling is quick and easy and works great with cucumbers, daikon, radishes, cabbage, carrots and more. The possibilities are endless!

---

3   cups thinly sliced vegetables of choice

¼   cup water

¼   cup brown rice vinegar

3   tablespoons sucanat

½   teaspoon sea salt

Place sliced vegetables in glass bowl and set aside.

In medium pot over high heat, combine water, vinegar, sucanat and salt. Bring to boil, reduce heat and simmer until sucanat dissolves. Remove from heat and cool 2–3 minutes. Pour over vegetables, cover and refrigerate. If liquid does not cover vegetables completely, stir every 30 minutes and continue marinating until vegetables break down and liquid covers all (about 2 hours). Store pickles refrigerated in pickling liquid in glass container.

Salad Dressings

WHEN I FIRST STARTED EATING WHOLE FOODS, someone suggested that I combine any cooked grain with legumes and vegetables, and toss them with my favorite salad dressing. Whether being used to spice up grains, legumes or a traditional salad, these dressings are sure to become staples in your refrigerator. I use a handheld blender for salad dressings to keep ingredients from separating, blend flavors and eliminate any chopping. If using a whisk, mince garlic and shallots first and then add to bowl with other ingredients. A sealable glass pitcher makes a perfect container for mixing and storing.

BASIC BALSAMIC VINAIGRETTE

1   garlic clove, peeled
1   small shallot
1   teaspoon lemon juice
2   tablespoons agave nectar
¼   cup balsamic vinegar
½   cup extra virgin olive oil
Sea salt and freshly ground
      black pepper to taste

Place all ingredients in bowl and emulsify with a handheld blender.

MAKES about 1 cup

GINGER SESAME VINAIGRETTE

1   small shallot
1   tablespoon grated
      fresh ginger
2   tablespoons tahini
¼   cup toasted sesame oil
¼   cup brown rice vinegar
¼   cup canola oil
1   tablespoon freshly
      squeezed orange
      or lime juice
1   teaspoon orange zest
2   tablespoons toasted
      hulled sesame seeds

Place all ingredients except sesame seeds in bowl and emulsify with handheld blender. Stir in sesame seeds.

MAKES about 1 cup

MAPLE MUSTARD VINAIGRETTE

1   garlic clove, peeled
1   heaping teaspoon
      prepared mustard
2   tablespoons maple syrup
1   tablespoon lemon juice
3   tablespoons red wine
      vinegar
½   cup extra virgin olive oil
Sea salt

Place all ingredients in bowl and emulsify with handheld blender.

MAKES about 1 cup

Julienned Beet, Broccoli Stem and Carrot Salad

THIS RAW SALAD IS FULL OF FLAVOR, COLOR AND TEXTURE and lends balance to a variety of menus, from light summer grilling to winter's heavier mixed grains and roasted tempeh.

---

1 raw golden beet, peeled and julienned

3 raw broccoli stems, peeled and julienned

2 carrots, julienned

1 cup cooked chickpeas

½ cup raisins

¼ cup chopped fresh parsley or cilantro

1 cup chopped toasted cashews

DRESSING

1 small shallot, minced

1 tablespoon lemon juice

2 tablespoons maple or honey mustard

2 tablespoons brown rice syrup

½ cup extra virgin olive oil

¼ teaspoon sea salt

Freshly ground black pepper

Combine beet, broccoli stems, carrots, chickpeas, raisins, and parsley or cilantro in large bowl. In separate bowl, combine dressing ingredients with whisk or handheld blender. Pour dressing over vegetables, toss to combine, top with toasted cashews and serve.

SERVES 6

Sautéed Garlic Greens

IF YOU'RE NEW TO EATING CLEAN, and don't know where to begin, start with something green. Green is one color of which we simply can't get enough! Dark leafy greens are full of chlorophyll, calcium and vitamins. Few other foods have their capacity to lift your mood, cleanse your liver and kidneys and balance blood pH.

---

2 bunches dark leafy greens (kale, collards, mustard greens, dandelion greens or chard)

3 garlic cloves, minced

2 tablespoons extra virgin olive oil

1 tablespoon mirin

Sea salt or ume plum vinegar

Remove dry stalk ends from greens and chop leaves into bite-size pieces. In Dutch oven or skillet over medium-low heat, sauté garlic in 1 tablespoon olive oil for 2–3 minutes until soft. Add greens and mirin and sauté 1 minute. Increase heat to medium, add water as needed to prevent sticking, cover and cook until greens break down. Remove from heat and toss with remaining tablespoon olive oil. Season to taste with salt or a few dashes of vinegar and serve.

SERVES 6

Ginger Sesame Greens

WHAT'S IMPORTANT ABOUT DARK LEAFY GREENS is not how you *prepare* them, but simply that you *eat* them! This is one of the simplest ways to prepare greens. With choices like this one and Sautéed Garlic Greens *(page 266),* you'll no longer need to skip over this section of the produce department.

---

2 bunches dark leafy greens (kale, collards, mustard greens, dandelion greens or chard)

1 tablespoon extra virgin olive oil

1 tablespoon grated fresh ginger

1 tablespoon mirin

1 tablespoon tamari

1 tablespoon toasted sesame oil

Toasted sesame seeds and sea salt or gomasio

Remove dry stalk ends from greens and chop leaves into bite-size pieces. In Dutch oven or skillet over medium heat, sauté ginger in olive oil, mirin and tamari for 1 minute. Add chopped greens, increase heat to medium-high, add water as needed to prevent sticking, cover and cook 3–5 minutes until greens are tender. Remove cover, toss greens to ensure even cooking and sauté 2–3 minutes longer. Turn off heat, drain excess cooking liquid and toss with toasted sesame oil. Sprinkle with gomasio or toasted sesame seeds and salt and serve.

SERVES 6

Sweet Potato and Black Bean Burritos with Cashew Cheese

I LOVE MEXICAN FOOD, and while I do not usually crave spicy foods, I find many spicy Mexican dishes to be surprisingly cooling as well. I am particularly sensitive to sugar, and sweet vegetables like root vegetables and tubers satisfy my need for sweets in a balanced way. Complete your menu by serving these burritos with Traditional Guacamole *(page 97)* and Tofu Sour Cream *(page 101)*.

CASHEW CHEESE
½   cup cashew pieces
¼   cup nutritional yeast
1   tablespoon canola oil

BURRITOS
3   sweet potatoes or yams
3   tablespoons lime juice
1½   cups cooked black beans
½   red onion, diced
1   large tomato, diced
8–10 soft corn tortillas
1½   cups prepared salsa
½   cup corn, fresh or frozen
¼   cup chopped scallions

Preheat oven to 400°F.

Place sweet potatoes on baking sheet or foil and bake 45 minutes or until soft. Remove from oven and cool.

PREPARING CASHEW CHEESE
In food processor, grind cashews to a fine meal. Add nutritional yeast and process briefly to combine. Add oil and process until you have a moist meal (do not overprocess or meal will become dough-like). Set aside.

ASSEMBLING
Set oven to broil. Place corn in strainer. Bring 1 cup water to boil and pour over corn to blanch or thaw.

Peel sweet potatoes and mash with lime juice. Fold in black beans, onion and tomato. Spoon filling into center of each tortilla, roll up and place, seam side down in shallow casserole. Spoon salsa over top and broil 3 minutes. Remove from broiler, top with cashew cheese and corn and broil 2 more minutes, watching closely to keep cheese from burning. Remove from broiler, top with chopped scallions and serve.

SERVES 8

Vegetable Nori Rolls

IF YOU DINE AT JAPANESE RESTAURANTS, you've likely encountered vegetables and rice wrapped in nori. Of all of the seaweeds, nori has the highest protein content and is the easiest to digest. These rolls make a great appetizer, snack or small meal. For even greater health benefits, substitute short grain brown rice for the sushi rice and increase your water to 4 cups.

---

2   cups sushi rice

3   cups water

Pinch of sea salt

2   tablespoons brown rice vinegar

2   tablespoons brown rice syrup

10   sheets toasted nori

1   small cucumber, julienned

1   carrot, julienned

1   avocado, peeled, pitted and cut into strips

ACCOMPANIMENTS

Shoyu or tamari

Pickled ginger

Wasabi paste

Combine rice, water and salt in large pot and bring to boil. Cover, then reduce heat and simmer 20 minutes or until all water is absorbed. Remove from heat and set aside to cool slightly.

In small saucepan, heat vinegar and rice syrup until dissolved, pour over rice and mix until combined. While rice is cooling, prepare vegetables.

ASSEMBLING NORI ROLLS

Place a sheet of nori, shiny side down, on work surface or bamboo rolling mat, with short edge facing you. Press a layer of rice ¼-inch thick along the edge of the sheet closest to you. Place vegetables in a long thin strip across the middle of the rice. Carefully fold the end of nori over the rice and continue rolling away from you to form a log. Moisten the edge with water to seal, and let sit briefly until nori is soft enough to cut easily. Cut into ½-inch pieces and arrange on platter. Serve with tamari, pickled ginger and wasabi.

SERVES 6

Quinoa with Sweet Corn

ORGANIC CORN IS READILY AVAILABLE in the freezer section of most grocery stores. I keep it in my freezer year-round which makes this recipe a breeze to put together. Quinoa takes only 15 minutes to cook which is just enough time to sauté some greens to complete your meal. This is also an easy way to perk up pan-roasted millet *(page 14)*.

1   cup quinoa
1½ cups water
Sea salt
1   tablespoon extra virgin olive oil
1   small onion, chopped
1½ cups corn, fresh or frozen
2   tablespoons chopped fresh parsley
Extra virgin olive oil or toasted sesame oil

Rinse and drain quinoa and place in pot with water and salt. Bring to boil, cover, reduce heat to low and simmer 15 minutes or until water is absorbed. Remove from heat and set aside to cool slightly before fluffing.

In large skillet or Dutch oven over medium heat, sauté chopped onion in olive oil until soft. Add corn and heat through. Fold in quinoa and parsley and drizzle with olive oil or toasted sesame oil. Season to taste with salt and serve.

SERVES 6

Quinoa Pilaf with Toasted Nuts and Seeds

THIS RECIPE COMES TOGETHER QUICKLY whether you're making it from scratch or doctoring up leftover quinoa (which is how this recipe originally came to be). Marinated onions are available in many natural food and gourmet stores and are even starting to make regular appearances in the cheese department of many conventional grocery stores. If you can't find them, substitute red onions. For variety, add fresh herbs, your favorite roasted vegetables or soaked and drained arame.

1	cup quinoa
1½	cups water or vegetable stock
¼	cup currants
½	cup marinated or roasted cipollini onions, quartered
¼	cup diced fennel
¼	cup toasted pumpkin seeds
¼	cup toasted sunflower seeds
¼	cup toasted sliced almonds
¼	cup chopped fresh cilantro or flat parsley
¼	cup extra virgin olive oil
2	teaspoons ume plum vinegar

Rinse and drain quinoa and place in pot with water or stock. Bring to boil, cover, reduce heat to low and simmer until all water is absorbed (about 15 minutes). Remove from heat and set aside to cool for a few minutes. Fluff with wooden spoon. Gently fold in currants, onions, fennel, pumpkin and sunflower seeds, almonds and cilantro or parsley. Drizzle with olive oil and vinegar and stir to combine. Serve warm or at room temperature.

SERVES 6

Brown Rice with Ginger and Umeboshi Plums

WHEN I FIRST DISCOVERED high-protein, non-gluten grains like quinoa and millet, I soon completely forgot about brown rice. Yet there is something so basic and simple about brown rice that recently I have found myself craving it, not only for its health benefits, satisfying taste and texture, but also for a return to pure and simple goodness.

1	cup short grain brown rice
2	cups water
1	thumb-size piece kombu
6	umeboshi plums
3	tablespoons brown rice vinegar
2	tablespoons brown rice syrup
¼	cup pickled ginger, minced
1	cup snow peas, trimmed, blanched and julienned

Soak rice for at least 1 hour in bowl with enough water to cover. Drain, rinse and place in pot with 2 cups water and kombu. Bring to boil, then reduce heat, cover and simmer for 25 minutes or until water is absorbed. Remove from heat, discard kombu and set rice aside.

To prepare umeboshi plums, remove pits and finely dice fruit. In small skillet over low heat, whisk together brown rice vinegar and syrup. Fold into rice along with plums, pickled ginger and peas and serve.

SERVES 6

Brown Rice Pudding

MY MOTHER HAS BEEN MAKING THIS RECIPE for as long as I can remember. In my home, we eat it for breakfast, lunch, dinner or dessert. It's also become quite popular at my children's school. We like it warm with a bit of cold rice milk poured over the top.

2½ cups cooked brown rice

12 ounces extra firm silken tofu

1 cup rice milk

¼ cup maple syrup

⅓ cup brown rice syrup

½ teaspoon nutmeg

2 teaspoons vanilla

1 tablespoon kudzu dissolved in 2 tablespoons rice milk

⅓ cup raisins

¼ cup semi-sweet dark chocolate chips

Ground cinnamon

Preheat oven to 350°F.

In food processor, combine cooked rice with tofu and rice milk. Add maple and brown rice syrups, nutmeg and vanilla and process to combine. Add dissolved kudzu and pulse to combine. Lightly oil 9 x 12-inch casserole and pour in mixture. Sprinkle top with raisins and chocolate chips and press down with a wooden spoon to incorporate into pudding. Sprinkle cinnamon evenly over top and bake 1 hour or until top is bubbling and browned. Remove from oven and cool slightly. Serve warm.

SERVES 8

Oatmeal Chocolate Chip (or Raisin) Cookies

I USUALLY FOLLOW MY OWN ADVICE when it comes to not keeping things in the house that I don't want to eat, and then one day it backfired on me. I simply had to have a cookie and it *had* to have chocolate in it. Within 20 minutes I was saved (and the rest of the family thanked me). If you prefer raisins, substitute them for the chocolate chips, or better yet, use both.

2	cups rolled oats
1	cup unbleached white flour or brown rice flour
¾	cup shredded unsweetened coconut
1	tablespoon ground cinnamon
¼	teaspoon sea salt
¾	cup maple syrup
½	cup canola oil
1	teaspoon vanilla extract
1	cup chopped toasted walnuts
½	cup semisweet dark chocolate chips or raisins

Preheat oven to 350°F.

In large bowl, combine oats, flour, coconut, cinnamon and salt. In separate bowl, whisk together syrup, oil and vanilla. Pour wet ingredients into dry and stir until evenly combined. Fold in walnuts and chocolate chips or raisins. Press dough into equal-size balls, place onto parchment-lined cookie sheet and bake 15 minutes or until lightly browned. Remove from oven – and do your best not to eat them all in one sitting!

MAKES 2 dozen

Teff Peanut Butter Chocolate Chip Cookies

IT SIMPLY DOESN'T MATTER HOW CLOSELY I follow my own dietary guidelines. When all is said and done, I still love cookies, and so do my children. Rather than deny ourselves, we came up with this decadent recipe that allows us to keep the wheat out of our diets but the cookies in.

1½ cups teff flour (preferably ivory)

¼ teaspoon sea salt

1 teaspoon baking soda

1 cup chunky 100% peanut butter

1 cup maple syrup

½ cup semisweet dark chocolate chips

Preheat oven to 350°F.

Combine all dry ingredients in one bowl and all wet ingredients in another. Pour wet ingredients over dry and blend until just combined – do not overmix. Fold in chocolate chips.

Line cookie sheet with parchment paper. Drop batter by heaping teaspoons onto cookie sheet. Leave cookies free-form or press down in crisscross pattern with tines of fork. Place in oven and bake 13 minutes or until lightly browned. The key to these cookies is not to overbake them! Remove from oven and place directly on wire rack to cool.

MAKES 20 cookies

Teff Ginger Molasses Cookies

TEFF IS SUCH A SMALL GRAIN that it is impossible to hull before grinding into flour, making its nutritional value nearly identical to that of the whole grain. These cookies are a high-protein, non-gluten, nutritious treat. Nobody will ever believe that they are made without wheat, eggs, milk, butter or brown sugar.

2	cups brown teff flour
1	teaspoon baking soda
¼	teaspoon sea salt
1	teaspoon ground cinnamon
¼	teaspoon ground cloves
½	teaspoon powdered mustard
½	cup almond butter
½	cup molasses
2	teaspoons tamari
1	tablespoon grated fresh ginger
½	cup maple syrup

Preheat oven to 350°F.

Combine all dry ingredients in large bowl and all wet ingredients in another. Pour wet ingredients over dry and blend until just combined – do not overmix.

Line cookie sheet with parchment paper. Drop batter by heaping teaspoons onto cookie sheet. There is no need to roll, flatten or shape mounds. Simply place in oven and bake 12 minutes. Remove from oven and place directly on wire rack to cool.

MAKES 24 cookies

ometimes the best place to start is at the very end. This index is a resource and a tool to help you turn Clean Food into delicious and nourishing meals. Select one new item each time you go to the grocery store or farmers market, and by the end of one year you will have significantly improved your diet with variety and nutritional value. Pick whatever catches your attention, look it up in this index and select the recipe that appeals to you. One item, one recipe and one choice at a time – these are the ingredients to make your kitchen the heart of a healthy home.

INDEX

Be nourished by the
fruits and beauty
of nature and make
every day a celebration
of the rhythms of the
seasons.

Terry